Pillars of Justice

PILLARS *of*
JUSTICE

Lawyers and the Liberal Tradition

OWEN FISS

▌▌▌

Harvard University Press

Cambridge, Massachusetts
London, England
2017

Library of Congress Cataloging-in-Publication Data
Names: Fiss, Owen M., author.
Title: Pillars of justice : lawyers and the liberal tradition / Owen Fiss.
Description: Cambridge, Massachusetts : Harvard University Press, 2017. |
Includes bibliographical references and index.
Identifiers: LCCN 2016040437 | ISBN 9780674971868 (hard cover : alk. paper)
Subjects: LCSH: Judges—United States. | Lawyers—United States. | Law
teachers—United States. | Civil rights—United States—History—20th century. |
Liberalism—United States—History—20th century. | Segregation in education—
Law and legislation—United States—History—20th century.
Classification: LCC KF371 .F57 2017 | DDC 340.092/273—dc23
LC record available at https://lccn.loc.gov/2016040437

To my grandchildren

Ezra Rubenfeld, Sophie Rubenfeld, Aidan Goldsmith,

Nicholas Palumbo, and Lucy Goldsmith

For the joy with which they infuse my life and for the promise

they bring to the world

Contents

III

The Fate of the Law

Coda

Pillars of Justice

Introduction

This book seeks to inspire and instruct. It portrays the lives of thirteen lawyers who, through their tireless devotion to justice, changed the world. These individuals have lived grandly in the law and in good part account for the course the law has taken over the past half-century. Their careers provide a source for understanding the dynamics responsible for the progress of the law and, even more, reveal what a life devoted to justice might entail.

Some of the lawyers portrayed in this book were crucially involved in the struggle for civil rights. One is Thurgood Marshall, who represented the petitioners in *Brown v. Board of Education* and later became a Justice of the Supreme Court. Another is William Brennan. Although Brennan did not join the Court until 1956, two years after the *Brown* ruling, he soon made evident his commitment to that decision and the liberal tradition to which it gave life. Two others—John Doar and Burke Marshall—led the Civil Rights Division of the Department of Justice during the turbulent 1960s and then shaped and implemented the civil rights policies of the federal government.

The liberalism associated with *Brown* has not been confined to the work of practitioners and judges; it has also been nourished and elaborated by the law teachers of the nation. Five of the greatest—Harry Kalven, Eugene Rostow, Arthur Leff, Catharine MacKinnon, and Joseph Goldstein—are portrayed in this book. Rostow was also the Dean of the Yale Law School from 1955 to 1965, during which time he recruited an extraordinary group of scholars—Rostow's Dozen—who would define the character of the Law School for a generation. MacKinnon, a student of mine at Yale and now a professor at the University of Michigan and at Harvard, has been a pioneer of feminist thought, seeking to extend to women the promise of equality that *Brown* had affirmed for Blacks. Each of these teachers has educated new generations of lawyers, and each in his or her own way determined what the law might become.

Law is an instrument of power, and as the history of implementing *Brown v. Board of Education* painfully revealed, judges must sometimes resort to the force made available to them by the law to implement their edicts. Law is, however, also an instrument of reason and depends for its legitimacy on the principled elaboration of public values. Many have struggled to find the right balance of power and reason in the law. The final section of the book deals with the lives and work of four lawyers who, over the years, made an enormous contribution, though from varied perspectives, to this quest. Two are scholars, Robert Cover of Yale and Morton Horwitz of Harvard; and two, Carlos Nino of Argentina and Aharon Barak of Israel, had careers that spanned teaching and practice.

Carlos Nino was a world-class legal philosopher who taught at the Universidad de Buenos Aires, while at the same time advising President Raúl Alfonsín of Argentina as he sought to end a brutal military dictatorship and restore democracy in that country. Barak was, as a young man, a professor of law in Israel and then Dean of the Law Faculty at Hebrew University. Later he served on the Israeli Supreme Court, first as a Justice, then as its President. Over his twenty-eight years on the Court, Barak handed down countless rulings celebrated throughout the world that indicated what respect for human rights requires.

I have known and worked closely with these lawyers. They were mentors, colleagues, friends. One was a student. Each had an important influence on my work, and each enriched my life immeasurably and accounted for much of the vibrancy of the law as I have known it and lived it. They are united by a deep, abiding commitment to *Brown v. Board of Education*, not as a formal legal precedent, as it indeed remains, but as an extraordinary moment in the life of the law, transforming the law into an instrument for realizing the highest ideals of the nation. The two lawyers from abroad, Nino and Barak, were of course not bound by *Brown* in any technical sense. Yet they, like scores of lawyers around the world, looked to *Brown* and the theory of law on which it rested as a beacon to guide them in their endeavors.

For those who worked in the American context, the commitment to *Brown* transcended ordinary political allegiances. Some were Republicans, others Democrats. Some were appointed to high office by Republican presidents, others by Democratic presidents. Some had no political affiliation whatsoever, or at least none of which I knew. What united these lawyers was not politics understood in a narrow, partisan way, but a dedication to the theory of *Brown*—a willingness, if need be, to move mountains to make certain that we were living up to our very best selves.

In dedicating his now famous 1980 book on the Supreme Court to Earl Warren—the Chief Justice and author of *Brown*—John Ely, once Dean of the Stanford Law School, wrote, "You don't need many heroes if you choose carefully." The choice of the persons portrayed in this book reflects my assessment of their importance to the progress of the law and to the triumphs of liberalism over the past half-century. It also reflects my belief, based on my lived experience, that their careers provide a standard by which to measure our own and guidance for anyone who wonders how he or she might achieve something in this world that is worthwhile and good.

I feel blessed by the fortuities of history that brought me together with these lawyers—people I think of as pillars of justice. In each chapter I describe the nature of my relationship with the person portrayed, sometimes colored by the deepest attachments. All biography is a form of autobiography, but in the accounts of others that I present here, the autobiographical element is explicit.

Although, as a youngster, I had toyed with the idea of a career in the law, when the Civil Rights Movement began to gather momentum I was headed in a different direction. From 1959 to 1961, I was a graduate student in philosophy at Oxford, one of the world's great centers of learning. My teachers—Gilbert Ryle, Isaiah Berlin, P. F. Strawson, H. L. A. Hart, and G. E. L. Owen—were among the very best Oxford had to offer, and they gave me a vivid sense of the challenges and excitement of philosophy. Yet the insular quality of the inquiries that then dominated the profession—for example, how can you be sure you are not dreaming?—made me restless, and I grew more restless as reports reached England about the civil rights protests back home. As history unfolded, John Kennedy won the 1960 presidential election, and the policies he soon announced opened new possibilities for public service. In light of these developments, I turned from philosophy and decided to study law.

I entered the Harvard Law School at a time when civil rights and the *Brown* ruling made only fleeting appearances in the curriculum, and even then not in an especially favorable light. In my final year, however, I enrolled in a seminar on constitutional litigation offered by Professor Paul Freund. Although the assigned material centered on the legal struggles of the New Deal, Freund encouraged me, in his kind, stately way, to pursue my vaguely formed inclinations and to write a paper on the implications of the *Brown* decision for the urban school systems of the North. In the course of that project, I spent considerable time in my final year at Harvard interviewing educators and civil rights leaders in the Boston area, which set me on the path that was to become my life's work.

After graduating in 1964, I clerked for Thurgood Marshall, who only a few years earlier had stepped down as Chief Counsel of the NAACP Legal Defense Fund to become a judge on the United States Court of Appeals for the Second Circuit. When that clerkship ended, we both headed for Washington—Marshall was appointed Solicitor General (which was to become a stepping stone for his appointment in 1967 to the Supreme Court), and I began a clerkship with Justice Brennan. While the docket of the Second Circuit during my clerkship with Marshall was largely occupied by issues arising from criminal prosecutions and complex commercial transactions, my year with Brennan focused primarily on cases involving the Civil Rights Act of 1964 and the Voting Rights Act of 1965.

It seemed only natural when I finished the Brennan clerkship that I should go to the Civil Rights Division of the Department of Justice. I worked there for two years as a special assistant to John Doar, then the Assistant Attorney General in charge of the Division. Before becoming Assistant Attorney General, Doar had served as First Assistant to Burke Marshall. In 1961, Marshall had been appointed by Attorney General Robert Kennedy to head the Division; to much acclaim, including from many who resisted *Brown,* he served in that position until the end of 1964. During the years that Doar and Marshall worked together, an extraordinary bond developed between the two, such that Marshall's presence was felt even during my years in the Division. I finally came to meet the legend in the spring of 1974, shortly before I joined the Yale faculty, and he remained a colleague and friend until his death in June 2003. The portraits of John Doar and Burke Marshall, together with those of Thurgood Marshall and William Brennan, form Part One of this volume, "The Struggle for Civil Rights."

In the summer of 1968, upon leaving the Civil Rights Division, I joined the law faculty of the University of Chicago. There I would begin another type of apprenticeship, this time with one of the preeminent legal scholars of his generation, Harry Kalven. By the time I arrived in Chicago, Kalven had distinguished himself as a torts teacher, as one of the authors of a famed, interdisciplinary study of the American jury, and above all, as a brave defender of political freedom. During the 1950s he was an outspoken critic of Senator Joseph McCarthy's witch hunt. Kalven is also widely celebrated for finding in the Supreme Court's 1964 decision in *New York Times Co. v. Sullivan* a new and more generous approach to freedom of speech. His 1964 book, *The Negro and the First Amendment*, hailed the Supreme Court decisions that protected the forceful and often dramatic protests of the Civil Rights Movement.

Kalven and I often taught together. Outside of class we chatted almost endlessly about the most recent Supreme Court decisions, about the unruly demonstrations that had occurred before the Democratic Convention in August 1968, shortly after I had arrived in Chicago, and about the protracted criminal trial of the leaders of the protest, a trial that was the subject of Kalven's long essay "Confrontation and Contempt." We also spoke about a book that he was writing on the history of freedom of speech in the United States. When he died in October 1974, Kalven left behind a thousand-page manuscript that his son Jamie edited, now and then with my advice. This work was eventually published in 1988 as *A Worthy Tradition*.

Kalven's liberalism was an exception for the Chicago faculty. For the most part, the Law School was dominated by conservative scholars. Two neoclassical economists, Aaron Director and Ronald Coase, were on its faculty when I first arrived in 1968. In 1969, Richard Posner joined the faculty, and he soon published his now famous treatise *Economic Analysis of Law*, in which he sought to demonstrate that the purpose of law is to promote efficiency. At the center of the constitutional law faculty was Philip Kurland, who in the foreword to the November 1964 *Harvard Law Review* used his vitriolic pen to excoriate the egalitarianism of the Court that was led by Earl Warren and responsible for *Brown*.

When I joined the Yale faculty in 1974, I found myself in a different milieu. A number of the Yale faculty, among them Robert Bork, were part of an insurgent conservative movement defined by its resistance to the egalitarianism of the 1960s. In fact, Bork was one of the most prominent leaders of this movement. He belittled much of the Warren Court's work, on occasion referring to the Equal Protection Clause, the provision of the Constitution that was the source of its egalitarianism, as the "Equal Gratification Clause."

In 1987, Bork was nominated to the Supreme Court by Ronald Reagan. That nomination was eventually turned back by the Senate, but only after a protracted and highly publicized hearing that centered on two articles written by Bork—a 1963 article in *The New Republic* opposing a bill that was about to become the Civil Rights Act of 1964, and a 1971 article in the *Indiana Law Journal* that denounced rulings of the Warren Court that afforded protection to artistic freedom and that, under the rubric of the right to privacy, had set aside a Connecticut law prohibiting the dissemination of information about contraceptives. This latter decision was a stepping stone to the 1973 decision in *Roe v. Wade* invalidating a Texas law criminalizing abortion.

At Yale, Bork was an exception. The Yale faculty was larger and more varied than Chicago's, and for the most part the school was a bastion of liberalism. A number of the faculty had worked on the briefs in *Brown*. Some, indeed, sprang to the defense of that decision once it came under attack in the academy. Students and faculty participated in the Civil Rights Movement, and graduates of the school were appointed to key positions in the Kennedy Justice Department. This group included, in addition to Burke Marshall, Byron White (Deputy Attorney General), John Douglas (head of the Civil Division), Louis Oberdorfer (head of the Tax Division), and Nicholas Katzenbach (head of the Office of Legal Counsel).

One of the singular figures on the Yale faculty was Eugene Rostow. Early in his career, Rostow achieved fame as the author of an article denouncing the 1944 *Korematsu* decision of the Supreme Court, which had upheld a wartime order of the federal government requiring all persons of Japanese ancestry, including U.S. citizens, to abandon their homes and jobs on the West Coast and move to internment camps located in the interior of the country. Strikingly, though, his critical assessment did not lead Rostow to lose faith in the Court as an instrument of public reason.

On the contrary, he wholeheartedly approved of *Brown* and the conception of judicial power that it embraced. Rostow served as Dean of the Yale Law School from 1955 to 1965, and the chapter about him here, "The Law according to Yale," describes the special character of the school that he helped build.

The Yale that I encountered when I arrived in New Haven in 1974 was not the work of any one person; nor did it follow a blueprint handed down on high. It was largely a product of intense, spontaneous interaction among strong-minded individuals, guided by norms that emerged over the decades and sharpened by students' demands and faculty's views about what was right for the students and their education. In addition to the accounts of Kalven and Rostow, Part Two, "Legal Education and the Culture of Liberalism," includes portraits of three figures at Yale who each had an enormous impact on the school and, for that matter, on the law itself: Arthur Leff, a near contemporary and once a colleague; Catharine MacKinnon, a student of mine in the 1970s; and Joseph Goldstein, one of the guiding spirits of the Law School for almost half a century.

Arthur Leff served on the Yale faculty for a tragically short period. He was appointed to the faculty in 1968 when he was in his early thirties, but died of lung cancer, at the age of forty-six, in 1981. He served during a trying period in the life of the school, a period that demanded his unique gifts of character and intellect. It was a time in which the Law School faculty suffered great losses and was confronted with an urgent need to rebuild.

During the late 1960s and early 1970s, several of Yale's most famous senior professors died, retired, or left for other schools. In addition, Robert Bork took an extended leave to serve in the Nixon and Ford administrations. Charles Reich, author of "The New Property" and *The Greening of America*, quit teaching law altogether. And most of the junior faculty were denied tenure and took positions elsewhere. In the face of these developments, the Yale faculty sprang into action and sought to recruit a new generation of law teachers, with the hope that they would seize the reins of the school. Leff was a member of this group of young scholars and soon became one of its leaders. He was a catalytic presence for the new generation, cheerfully prodding us on with his wit and countless acts of graciousness, helping to make us the best professors we could possibly be. He also provided an example to be emulated.

Leff was a supremely popular professor, greatly admired by his students. He taught contracts and achieved prominence in that field, but his intellectual curiosity was virtually unbounded. He offered sharply varied courses and in a number of famous articles attacked Posner's view of law as nothing more than an instrument of economic efficiency. Leff saw the aim of law as justice rather than efficiency, and he identified an array of disciplines, beyond economics, that bore on the questions of what justice required and how it might be achieved.

Catharine MacKinnon was a student at the Law School during the 1970s. Even then, she was at the forefront of the women's movement. Her law school paper on the sexual harassment of working women was turned into a book that was published by Yale University Press in 1979, only two years after she graduated. Guided by the same insistent demand for equality announced in *Brown*, MacKinnon gained even greater prominence analyzing social practices such as prostitution and pornography, and calling on lawmakers to curtail these practices.

MacKinnon's view of pornography appeared to some to be in conflict with a central precept of the liberal tradition, given forceful expression by the Warren Court, that sought to curb the censorship of great works of art and literature because they were sexually explicit. In truth, however, MacKinnon sought to deepen our understanding of liberalism, not to repudiate it; her point was that the bombardment of our culture by the pornography industry threatened to turn women into sexual objects, thereby perpetuating their subordination and impairing their capacity to participate fairly and fully in public debate.

MacKinnon's work dramatically broadened the perspective of many liberals, myself included, who were committed not only to freedom of speech but also to equality. Guido Calabresi, Dean of the Yale Law School from 1985 to 1994, now a federal judge, often spoke of the special pleasure a teacher experiences in learning from a student. The pleasures to which Calabresi referred are compounded many times over when a student educates a teacher, as MacKinnon did, by founding a wholly new field of study.

Joseph Goldstein was a true iconoclast and as strong-minded a colleague as one might ever encounter. He joined the Yale faculty in the late 1950s as one of the dozen appointed during Rostow's deanship. Goldstein taught at Yale until his death in March 2000, at the age of seventy-six. He taught primarily criminal law and family law and was a pioneer in exploring how the insights of psychoanalysis could be applied to the formulation of rules for governing society. Together with two of the world's most famous analysts, Anna Freud and Albert Solnit, Goldstein wrote *Beyond the Best Interests of the Child*, a 1973 book on custody disputes that was heralded by both the academy and the bar.

Aside from his scholarly achievements, Goldstein was relentless in his efforts to preserve the unwritten rules that governed Yale and endowed the school with its unique outlook on law and legal education. At the heart of these efforts was a belief, manifested by his own behavior, that the institution and its administration should have no control over what a professor wrote or taught. He insisted on protecting the autonomy of each individual faculty member, so much so that it would not be a stretch to say that he felt that each professor was endowed with a measure of sovereignty.

Part Three of this book, "The Fate of the Law," features four lawyers whose careers, especially when considered collectively, reveal the fault lines within the liberal tradition. This tradition, at least in its classic form, posits the existence of a line separating law from politics and then places decisions such as *Brown* on the side of the law on the theory that they constitute reasoned elaborations of constitutional principles. Liberals also recognize, however, that the judiciary is part of the apparatus of the state and that, as a result, it is subject to dynamics—some arising from the appointments process, some from the need to implement judicial edicts—that routinely test the law's commitment to reason by introducing into the law the unpredictable forces of practical politics.

I encountered the challenge of navigating the boundary between law and politics in my clerkships and in my years working in the Civil Rights Division. I also reflected on it throughout my academic career. Yet this challenge arose in a new and startling manner in June 1985, when I traveled to Argentina to witness an extraordinary event in world history—the heroic, almost quixotic effort of a newly elected president, unaided by a conquering army, to place the highest officers of Argentina's armed forces on trial for human rights abuses that they had committed during a brutal military dictatorship that lasted from 1976 to 1983.

This trip to Argentina had a profound impact on my thinking, due in no small measure to the special relationship I developed with Carlos Nino. He was perhaps the most important legal philosopher ever to come from Latin America, and at the time we met he was serving as President Alfonsín's adviser on human rights policies. In 1987, he became a regular visiting professor at Yale, where he deepened and extended his interest in constitutional law. In August 1993, Nino, only forty-nine, died while on a trip to Bolivia to work on that country's Constitution. Chapter 10, "The Death of a Public Intellectual," describes the circumstances of the tragedy as well as Nino's philosophy and his role in the 1985 Buenos Aires trial against the military junta.

Even as a presidential adviser, Nino lived in the kingdom of ideas. Law for him was all reason. Robert Cover, a Yale colleague and a close friend of mine (who also died young, at the age of forty-two), took a very different view of the matter. When I first joined the Yale faculty, Cover and I joined forces to revise the traditional first-year procedure course. In 1979, we published *The Structure of Procedure*, a collection of essays that outlined the essential terms of the revision we were contemplating. We then settled down, largely thanks to the prodding of Judith Resnik, to finish a casebook on the subject (eventually published two years after Cover's 1986 death).

In 1983, Cover's work took a different and more theoretical turn when he published his now legendary *Harvard Law Review* article *"Nomos* and Narrative," putting forth a theory of law that emphasized its violent character. Cover began his theory by focusing on the norms of local, tightly bound communities and then proceeded to characterize the action of the nation-state and its judges as "jurispathic" because, he said, they killed all of the local norms but one in order to create the supreme law of the land. Judges, Cover proclaimed, are people of violence. In highlighting the element of violence in his account of law, Cover put into question not just liberal theory in general, but also the defense of *Brown* offered by liberals who insisted on viewing that ruling as an exercise in public reason.

As a personal matter, there could be no doubt about Cover's commitment to the egalitarianism of *Brown*. During his undergraduate days at Princeton, Cover traveled to Albany, Georgia, to participate in the civil rights demonstrations taking place there. Early in his teaching career Cover published a widely acclaimed book on the law of slavery, *Justice Accused*. In fact, when I first met Cover in the early 1970s he was teaching in a summer program in New York that was aimed at preparing Black students already admitted to law school for what they might encounter in the months ahead. But by emphasizing the violent dimensions of law and by characterizing the judge's work as essentially jurispathic, Cover departed from the account of *Brown* that sought to ground its legitimacy in the reason of the law. What legitimated *Brown,* according to Cover, were the political commitments of the Justices—their abhorrence of Jim Crow and the willingness to use the coercive power at their disposal to enforce their will. *Brown* was, for Cover, a political act and should be judged on those terms.

Starting in the mid-1970s, a new movement took root in the American legal academy—Critical Legal Studies (CLS). The method of analysis employed by proponents of CLS differs sharply from Cover's, but they too insist on the centrality of power and politics in the law, proudly proclaiming that "law is politics." In speaking of "politics" in this way, the proponents of CLS refer not to the ordinary partisan conflicts between, for example, Democrats and Republicans, but to the broadly conflicting views about the nature of the good that divide society. Law, according to this school of thought, represents a triumph of one view of the good over another and is not the product of transcendent reasoning. What endows one view of the good as opposed to any other with the mantle or authority of law, according to CLS, is nothing more than the way power is eventually distributed—who controls the machinery of the state and is thus able to declare what the law is.

Like liberals, the proponents of CLS are committed to the egalitarianism of *Brown*. Unlike liberals, though, they do not see that decision as the unfolding of public reason or, as some liberals proclaim, an interpretation of equal protection that is both objective and true. Rather, *Brown*, they insist, merely reflects the outcome of ceaseless struggles for power and endows with the authority of the law the beliefs of those who happened to possess power at that historical moment. In time, this power might shift to, or be seized by, another group, one less committed to the egalitarianism of *Brown*, as it did upon the retirement of Earl Warren and the transfer of power in the 1970s to another bloc of Justices, led by William Rehnquist, who were, at least by then, prepared to leave the precedent on the books, but nonetheless determined to drain that decision of all its generative power. Those who attacked *Brown* might well be resisted—not, however, on the theory that they have betrayed the law, but because of the moral offensiveness of their views.

Harvard Law School was the epicenter of CLS when it first emerged, and its leadership then belonged to three professors: Roberto Unger, Duncan Kennedy, and Morton Horwitz. As chance would have it, Horwitz is a close friend from my high school days who achieved renown as a legal historian. His acclaimed first book, *The Transformation of American Law: 1780–1860*, advanced the view that in the early nineteenth century the propertied classes manipulated key legal doctrines, like tort and contract law, to their advantage. In the 1990s, Horwitz turned to *Brown* and the other decisions that gave life to the liberal tradition. In this context Horwitz was much more upbeat, but only by developing a theory that, in the spirit of CLS, eradicated, or at least blurred, the line between law and politics. Specifically, in his view, the rise of the Warren Court coincided with the ascendancy during the twentieth century of a political ideal—democracy—that became widely shared among the nation's powerful interests, and that in turn was broadly served by *Brown*'s egalitarianism. In this way Horwitz saved *Brown* but, I fear, lost the law.

In the chapter about Horwitz I try to restore reason to the place it properly deserves in the law. For that purpose I draw on the theoretical work of Aharon Barak, a professor, a judge, and a man who, as a Holocaust survivor and an Israeli, knows violence firsthand. Barak started teaching regularly at the Yale Law School during the 1980s, when he was a Justice on the Supreme Court of Israel. Initially, he participated in the seminar "The Limits of Law," which was then being taught by Joseph Goldstein and Burke Marshall—a strange arrangement I first thought, since Barak's decisions always emphasized the potential of the law, not its limits. But as I soon discovered, the contrasting perspectives enriched the seminar, and Barak's involvement in it led him to develop close relationships with the Yale faculty and the Law School in general.

Aharon Barak became the President of the Israeli Supreme Court in 1995 and retired in 2006 when he turned seventy. Since his retirement, he has continued to teach at Yale and in Israel, publishing such important works as *The Judge in a Democracy, Purposive Interpretation in Law, Proportionality,* and most recently, *Human Dignity.* The work of this extraordinary jurist—a professor-turned-judge-turned-professor— shows in great detail the full but unadorned place of reason in the law. He gave life to human rights as a subject of judicial protection; and much like Nino's, Barak's emphasis on the reason of the law offered a much-needed antidote to the jurisprudence of Cover and Horwitz.

In conversation, Barak often spoke admiringly of *Brown,* as though it provided a standard by which to measure himself and his work. It was as though *Brown,* in its pristine force, had found a new home. As a formal matter, of course, Barak spoke only for Israel, but his body of rulings has become what *Brown* once was—a beacon for all the world. These rulings are instructive in many domains, but none with more urgency today than in confronting the threat of terrorism. On numerous occasions Barak pointed out (turning an ancient adage on its head) that when the cannons roar the law must not fall silent. Borrowing an expression of his, I have called the chapter on Barak "Law Is Everywhere."

Throughout this book I focus on the lives of others. I describe their achievements and their impact on the law, sometimes as practitioners and sometimes as teachers. In these essays my views on the practice of law and legal education emerge, but only incidentally (more or less). The book's Coda, "Toiling in Eden," is derived from an address that I gave at the Law School's 2011 graduation as I was about to retire. In it I speak directly and forthrightly about the Yale Law School and my place in it and describe the ambitions that guided my teaching for over forty years. In concluding, I acknowledge the worries that I carry about the condition of the world that we find ourselves in, and about the difficulties, now that *Brown* has been drained of much of its meaning, of achieving justice in it. In the end, though, I invoke a Yale tradition that might put these concerns into perspective and lead me to be more upbeat. This tradition locates the golden age in American law in the past, criticizes the present for failing to meet those standards, and then predicts that another golden age is about to rise.

I

THE STRUGGLE FOR
CIVIL RIGHTS

Thurgood Marshall on the steps of the Supreme Court in the spring of 1955, perhaps soon after he argued the remedial phase of *Brown v. Board of Education*. The arguments were presented to the Court from April 11 to 14, 1955; the decision was handed down on May 31, 1955; and this photograph appeared in the June 1, 1955, issue of *Life* magazine. Marshall's expression suggests a premonition that the Court would not order the desegregation process to commence immediately, as he had argued it should, but with "all deliberate speed."

1

Thurgood Marshall

The Law's Promise

In the mid-1950s, when I was a senior at Stuyvesant High School in Manhattan, a group of us traveled to Washington, D.C., during our spring
vacation. We made the rounds of the monuments and one morning
decided to visit the Supreme Court. We waited in the line for visitors
and eventually were ushered in to the grand, almost majestic chamber.

As it turned out, we entered in the middle of an oral argument. We
did not fully understand what was transpiring, but no one could miss
the drama that was then unfolding. A tall Black lawyer—set in a sea
of white faces—was addressing the Justices, and all eyes were fixed
on him. The lawyer spoke with a special eloquence. He was dignified
and proper, he stood tall and straight, but his words were accessible to
all. His case was put in simple, clear, and powerful words. Those words
were uttered with patience, and with a steely, almost icy calm, yet be-
neath them was an urgency that could not help but move the audience.
The moment was electrifying.

Afterward I learned that this argument was part of the proceedings
of *Brown v. Board of Education* and that the lawyer standing before the

Court was Thurgood Marshall. It was April 1955, and the Justices had turned to the question of remedy.

In the fall of 1963 Thurgood Marshall and I met once again, this time face to face. I was in my last year at the Harvard Law School, and by then Marshall had become a Judge on the Second Circuit Court of Appeals. Thanks to the generosity of Benjamin Kaplan, one of the giants on the Harvard faculty and one of Marshall's devoted admirers, I was sent to the Judge's chambers in Foley Square for a clerkship interview. I was to meet one of the heroes of my youth and, if I was lucky, work closely with him for a year after graduation

I walked into Marshall's chambers and first met Fred Halsey, the young bailiff who was studying law at night, and Alice Stovall, the Judge's secretary. They calmed me down—well, as much as anyone could—and then I was shown into the Judge's office. He was sitting at the end of his library table; he hardly ever sat behind his desk. His jacket was off. He wore a white shirt, long-sleeved, and the kind of tie that one should only wear under a judicial robe (it was about six inches too short for such a tall man). Marshall played with his mustache, shuffled the many papers on the table, looked over the top of his glasses, and then began one of the most remarkable conversations of my life.

I cannot remember what I said, or even if I said anything. I do, however, remember his teasing me about my Harvard education. He referred to Harvard with a respectful disdain and then asked if I could write short, pithy memorandums like those of Jerome Frank. Before his appointment to the Second Circuit, Frank had been on the Yale faculty and was one of the leaders of Legal Realism—the school of thought that advanced the unremarkable proposition that judges are people and are subject to the same impulses that govern all of us. Marshall summarized one of Frank's memorandums for me, and I dare not repeat that summary in public, although I acknowledge that the memorandum itself was short.

In that first conversation, Marshall extolled the position that "my" dean—Erwin Griswold, then Dean of the Harvard Law School—had taken when asked by a southern Senator what he thought about a memorandum opposing pending civil rights legislation. "I would give it a C," Dean Griswold had replied. Marshall then explained with wry amusement one of his initial encounters in the courthouse. When he was first looking for his chambers, a bailiff asked if he was the electrician. "No way," Marshall had replied, "I could never get into their union." He chuckled at that, and the stories continued, his accent changing several times, and his hearty laughter filling the office. Some days later the offer came; I wanted to accept on the spot, but in order to avoid an impulsive decision, he made me wait a few days.

I began the clerkship at the end of the summer of 1964. I never dared tell the Judge how I idolized him; expressions of admiration always seemed out of place ("knucklehead" was the closest to a compliment that Marshall paid his clerks). Each day seemed more thrilling than the previous one. One morning, after racing to chambers, I went to his office to discuss (or maybe even argue about) a pending case. I approached Marshall at his large writing table, and he glanced up at me. The excitement that I felt was palpable, and it was only during a brief pause in the conversation that I looked down and noticed my pajamas coming through the bottom of my slacks. I gulped, and then struggled to continue, not knowing whether the Judge had noticed the telltale sign of the excessive eagerness of a twenty-six-year-old.

In 1964 the Second Circuit was perhaps the nation's most influential court—at least in the eyes of my Harvard mentors. My law school classes had been filled with references to the other greats of the Circuit, not just Jerome Frank, but also Charles Clark, Thomas Swan, Augustus Hand, and above all, Learned Hand. Benjamin Kaplan's course on copyright, in particular, was largely a celebration of Learned Hand, so much so that when I began my clerkship and glanced over the directory of offices, I was half surprised to find Hand no longer on the bench.

Even though it was deeply respected, the Circuit was also divided, and on a number of important occasions Marshall found himself disagreeing with his colleagues. In the main, this disagreement centered not on civil rights cases, but rather on the rights of the accused in criminal proceedings, or more specifically, on a number of decisions the Supreme Court had recently handed down, decisively enlarging those rights: *Mapp v. Ohio*, *Gideon v. Wainwright*, *Fay v. Noia*, and *Escobedo v. Illinois* (leading to *Miranda v. Arizona*).

Some of the Judges on the Second Circuit, particularly those who had held positions of leadership in the bar and the academy, accepted these Supreme Court rulings in the most grudging fashion. Marshall took a different view. He insisted that these decisions be taken at their full value, not out of blind obedience to the authority of the Supreme Court, but because such rulings represented a constitutional promise fulfilled. Once, Marshall even took issue with a Supreme Court ruling on double jeopardy from another era, the 1910 decision in *Brantley v. Georgia*. He refused to follow that decision, and in that sense "overruled" it on the assumption that the Supreme Court itself would repudiate the precedent once it had an occasion to address the issue again. (As it turns out, he was right.)

Yet while Marshall often took such bold stands, he always did so with a measure of unease. It was no fun for a new Judge, one whose appointment took the Senate almost a year to confirm, and one who had no ties to the "white shoe" law firms of Wall Street, to raise his voice in protest against the prominent, the established, and the well-recognized—or against people he liked and respected. Yet he was dedicated to doing what he believed right and drew on the very same quality of character— courage—that sustained him for over thirty years as a civil rights lawyer, as he crisscrossed the South in pursuit of Jim Crow, moving, as each of his many stories made evident, from one hair-raising incident to the next.

In July 1965, as my year with him was drawing to a close, a call came from President Lyndon Johnson. I was dispatched to where the Judge was having lunch, interrupted him, and eagerly reported: "The President called." Looking up, he responded, somewhat gruffly: "The president of what?" As it turned out, Johnson wanted to appoint him Solicitor General of the United States. It was not an easy decision. His wife, knowing the family finances, openly worried whether they could afford to move to Washington. But no one, absolutely no one, could say no to LBJ, so Thurgood Marshall resigned from the Second Circuit and became Solicitor General. I too moved to Washington, to begin another clerkship, this one with Justice William Brennan.

Arriving in Washington at about the same time as the Marshalls, my wife, Irene, and I were lucky enough to be invited to Marshall's swearing-in and afterwards to join the Marshall family in the Oval Office for a brief meeting with the President. I had spent a great deal of my clerkship with the Judge listening to his stories; often I had to work late into the night to catch up on my assignments. But Marshall paled against Johnson as a raconteur. The President sat behind his desk and proceeded to tell one story after another, most of them jovial, showering the Marshalls with warmth and friendship. A nice welcome to Washington.

While clerking for Brennan, I often watched Marshall in his new role as Solicitor General from the "guest box" in the courtroom, in much the same way that a student might follow an inspiring and beloved teacher from one public appearance to another. I had changed, and Marshall had changed, yet I could not help but think back to the first time that I saw Marshall in that majestic chamber of the Supreme Court in April 1955. He still stood tall, but now he was wearing tails (the formal attire of the Solicitor General). Now he was cordially addressed by the Chief Justice as "General." Now Marshall read his argument, until pressed by one of the Justices, usually in the most cordial way, and this feature of his presentation, plus the fact that he was now speaking for the government, lessened the sense of drama in the courtroom. Over the course of a decade, America had also changed. We had already witnessed the great demonstrations of the Civil Rights Movement—the Freedom Rides, protests on the streets of Birmingham, the March on Washington, Freedom Summer, and the March from Selma to Montgomery. Congress responded to these events and to the larger teachings of the Supreme Court by enacting the Civil Rights Act of 1964 and the Voting Rights

Act of 1965, thereby extending and deepening the national commitment to *Brown* and what Marshall had wrought.

In March 1967, President Johnson named Ramsey Clark as Attorney General, which, to no one's surprise, immediately led to the announcement by Tom Clark, Ramsey's father, who was only sixty-seven, that he would retire from the Supreme Court at the end of the current Term. He stepped down on June 12. On the very next day, President Johnson—the great choreographer—nominated Thurgood Marshall, who had now served for two years as his Solicitor General, to fill Justice Clark's place on the Court. On August 30, 1967, the Senate confirmed Marshall's nomination by a vote of 69 to 11. Marshall took his seat on the bench when the new Term began in October. At that point Judge Marshall became Justice Marshall.

The appointment of Thurgood Marshall to the Supreme Court was a transcendent moment in the history of the United States. It was also a moment of joy for Marshall and liberal advocates. This elation did not, however, last long. Owing to a number of events—the escalation of the Vietnam War, President Johnson's decision in March 1968 not to run for reelection, and the assassination in June 1968 of Robert Kennedy, the leading Democratic contender—Hubert Humphrey, Johnson's Vice President, was chosen to run against Richard Nixon in the 1968 election, and he lost. Nixon had campaigned against the increasingly unpopular Vietnam War. He also attacked many of the landmark decisions of the Supreme Court rendered during the Chief Justiceship of Earl Warren. In the first three years of his presidency, Nixon found himself in a position to make a number of appointments to the Supreme Court— Warren Burger, Harry Blackmun, William Rehnquist, and Lewis Powell—that radically altered its direction.

Soon Justice Marshall began to feel under siege. In 1970, after the personnel on the Court began to change, Marshall was hospitalized with pneumonia, and, as he told the story, was informed by a doctor in the hospital that President Nixon had been eagerly inquiring about his health. Instantly, Marshall instructed the doctor to tell the President, "Not yet."

Fortunately, Marshall proved true to his word; he soon recovered and returned to work. His resolve, however, meant that he would spend the next twenty years—almost his entire career on the Supreme Court—in battle against the conservative assault on *Brown* and its progeny.

On Justice Marshall's retirement, a professor trying to summarize Marshall's years of service on the Court lightheartedly referred to him as "the Great Dissenter," a reference to predecessors like Oliver Wendell Holmes and before him, John Marshall Harlan. In his dissents, Marshall continually tried to remind us how far short we had fallen from our ideals. Some of the most striking dissents came in school cases. In almost all of the major school desegregation cases from *Milliken v. Bradley* in 1974 to *Board of Education v. Dowell* in 1991, Marshall was on the losing side, and he rightly complained that the majority had broken faith with *Brown*. As he warned in *Milliken*, "Unless our children begin to learn together, there is little hope that our people will ever learn to live together."

Marshall's dissents were not confined to school desegregation cases; his protests extended to all manner of cases involving the Bill of Rights and the Civil War amendments. He decried the dismantling of procedural protections for the accused, the erection of new barriers to affirmative action, the criminalization of unpopular speech, and the reinstitution of the death penalty. Perhaps fittingly, on his last day on the bench, Justice Marshall dissented from a Rehnquist decision permitting the admission of victim impact evidence in capital cases, concluding his opinion and his career on this worrisome note: "Cast aside today are those condemned to face society's ultimate penalty. Tomorrow's victims may be minorities, women, or the indigent."

Although Marshall was a warm and jovial person, his frustration with the direction of the Supreme Court during the 1970s and 1980s would sometimes slip through. An early example occurred in 1973 in *United States v. Kras,* in which a majority upheld a statute requiring filing fees even as it was applied to impoverished litigants. Noting that the statute allowed the payment of the fees in installments ranging from $1.28 to $1.92

a week, the majority opinion, written by Harry Blackmun, dismissed any claim of hardship on the ground that the fees seemed only a slight burden, "less than the price of a movie and little more than the cost of a pack or two of cigarettes." Justice Marshall responded angrily: "It is perfectly proper for judges to disagree about what the Constitution requires. But it is disgraceful for an interpretation of the Constitution to be premised upon unfounded assumptions about how people live."

Such angry protests became more common as the retrenchment of rights became more pronounced. By his later years he would come to describe various majority positions as "astonishing," "arrogant," "facile," "myopic," "perfunctory," "impetuous," "dismaying," and "indecent." In 1989, Marshall used almost all of these adjectives in a single dissent, when the majority—now consisting of the three relatively new Reagan appointees (Sandra Day O'Connor, Anthony Kennedy, and Antonin Scalia), as well as William Rehnquist, Byron White, and John Paul Stevens—invalidated an affirmative action program in Richmond, Virginia, that gave minority-owned businesses a modest preference in awarding municipal contracts. Marshall complained that the country was not "anywhere close to eradicating racial discrimination or its vestiges" and that in suggesting otherwise the majority was "constitutionalizing its wishful thinking" and doing "a grave disservice not only to those victims of past and present racial discrimination in this Nation whom government has sought to assist, but also to this Court's long tradition of approaching issues of race with the utmost sensitivity."

Over the course of his life, such displays of anger were the exception. Thurgood Marshall was a passionate man, but he was strongly disciplined. He worked steadily and determinedly to forge the law into an effective instrument of reform, and in doing so he always listened to his adversaries, pondered their arguments, and then patiently set forth reasons for his disagreement. This was his way on the Court as well as during his years as an advocate. Justice Hugo Black once described Marshall's argument in the *Brown* case in just these terms. He contrasted Marshall's performance with that of John W. Davis—reputed by some to be the greatest advocate of his day—who, in representing South Carolina, lost both his cool and his argument when he crossed swords with Marshall.

On many occasions the Justice assured his friends that he would never retire from the Supreme Court. He said that he intended to continue for the full term of his office, which, he reminded us, was for life. "I expect to die at 110, shot by a jealous husband," he would quickly add. Those familiar with his bravado, and who saw the toll of age, were not surprised by his decision to step down in 1991, for he was then eighty-three and had served twenty-four years on the Court. But many were deeply saddened by his retirement, for it seemed to spell the end, the very end, of an era, the culmination of a decline begun some twenty years before, when Earl Warren, Hugo Black, William Douglas, and Abe Fortas had stepped down and were replaced by appointees of Presidents Richard Nixon and Gerald Ford. This process of changing the personnel of the Court continued through the Reagan years, and in 1990, during the presidency of George H. W. Bush, Marshall's beloved colleague and friend William Brennan retired. Thus, with Marshall went the last of those Justices who were part of the governing coalition of the Warren Court and who gave that Court its unique place in history. Marshall was also the lawyer responsible for the initial victory in *Brown*, and thus his decision to withdraw from public life underscored in a bold and dramatic way the troubled state of the legacy of the Warren Court and, for that matter, American law in general. Marshall died in 1993.

Throughout his life, Thurgood Marshall was moved and supported by his love of family. In December 1955, following the death of his first wife, he married Cecilia Suyat, known to everyone as Cissy, and they soon had two sons. Cissy was spirited and determined, but also exuded the warmth that was the Justice's trademark. Every time Marshall said—which was quite often—"Isn't she something?," all who knew her rushed to agree. Marshall was equally devoted to his sons. He certainly was the only judge on the Second Circuit who drove his children to and from school each and every day—and enjoyed it. He also got a kick out of the fact that his younger son, John, had become, in the Justice's words, "a law enforcement officer." At the time of Marshall's retirement, John was a Virginia state trooper; later he would become a U.S. Marshal and still later, Secretary of Public Safety in Virginia. Marshall's older son, Thurgood Jr., followed more closely in the Justice's footsteps: He became a lawyer. On his last day of service, Marshall stepped from behind the bench, took off his robe, walked to the Supreme Court lectern he knew so well, and moved Thurgood Jr.'s admission to the bar. This small ceremony, and Cissy's presence in the courtroom on the final day of Justice Marshall's tenure, spoke powerfully of the role of his family in his life.

In the late 1920s, Marshall had announced that he would make his life in the law. Amid the brutal and all-encompassing racism of the day, his grandmother responded to this announcement by offering, with only a touch of irreverence, to teach him how to cook so that he might always have a job to support himself. Marshall did, in fact, become an excellent cook (his crab gumbo was the best I ever tasted), but his legal career flourished in a way that his grandmother could have never imagined, making him the most accomplished lawyer of the twentieth century: Chief Counsel of the NAACP Legal Defense Fund, Judge on the Court of Appeals for the Second Circuit, Solicitor General of the United States, Justice of the Supreme Court. At the heart of all these endeavors was a love of the law—not just because of the maneuvering of which he, always imbued with the instincts of a trial lawyer, never seemed to tire—but more important, because of the law's redemptive possibilities. For Marshall, the law was a source of radical hope. It has a unique capacity to help us realize what is best in ourselves, and he saw it as the only institution with a fair chance of eradicating the racial caste system that had long marred our history.

Just after his retirement from the Court, Marshall was asked by a reporter how he wanted to be remembered. Referring to himself in the third person, the Justice answered with the spontaneity and immediacy that belong to the deepest truths: "That he did what he could with what he had." Marshall was a man of enormous, almost miraculous, accomplishments, and in summing up his life in this way, he revealed the self-effacing modesty that made him so endearing, and that infused younger generations with hope and purpose. Thurgood Marshall toiled in the profession for sixty years and will always remain a monument to all that is good in it. As long as there is law, his name will be remembered, and when his story is told, all the world will listen.

William Brennan in October 1986, four years before his retirement from the Supreme Court.

2

William Brennan

A Life Lived Twice

William Brennan died on July 24, 1997, at age ninety-one. Seven years earlier, when he stepped down from the Supreme Court after serving for thirty-four years, he was showered with accolades and honors and treated as a national hero. With the possible exception of the send-off enjoyed by Justice Oliver Wendell Holmes, the celebration of Brennan surrounding his retirement was unmatched in the history of the Court.

At the moment of the Justice's retirement, my feelings were mixed. I rejoiced in Brennan's glory, feeling that the honors were so well deserved; I also felt a touch of sadness, for the Justice who so loved his work and even more for the law that he helped to craft. I sensed that Brennan's retirement would imperil the achievements of the Warren Court in new and profound ways. Sadly, the past twenty-five years of Supreme Court history have confirmed this fear.

The Warren Court refers to that extraordinary phase of Supreme Court history that began in 1953 with President Dwight Eisenhower's appointment of Earl Warren as Chief Justice. Brennan joined that Court near its beginning, in 1956. In those early years, Warren and Brennan drew on the support of Hugo Black and William Douglas, who had been on the Court since the 1930s. This group turned into a solid majority in 1962, when Felix Frankfurter retired and President John Kennedy filled his vacancy with Arthur Goldberg. In 1965, President Lyndon Johnson appointed Goldberg as Ambassador to the United Nations and filled the resulting vacancy on the Supreme Court with another liberal, Abe Fortas. Thurgood Marshall's appointment in 1967 added to the strength of the coalition, and this majority of five (six after 1967) was occasionally able to pick up the vote of Potter Stewart or Byron White, or even that of John Harlan, a conservative who often found himself bound by stare decisis. It was in those halcyon days of the Warren Court, the October 1965 Term, that I clerked for Justice Brennan.

Like everything else, law always has an antecedent. The roots of the Warren Court's jurisprudence can be found in earlier periods, especially in the decisions of the Supreme Court in the 1930s that gave new life to the principle guaranteeing freedom of speech, thereby elevating the earlier dissents of Oliver Wendell Holmes and Louis Brandeis to majority status. In this period the Court also began to ensure a modicum of procedural fairness in criminal prosecutions. Yet there was something distinctive and special about the Warren Court—almost a new beginning.

This break with the past was signaled by the ruling in *Brown v. Board of Education*, which was handed down almost as soon as Warren took his place on the bench. The Court declared that segregated schools can never be equal, and in so doing undertook the most challenging of all constitutional tasks: making good on the nation's promise of racial equality. The Court's ruling in *Brown* was premised on a conception of law and a set of commitments that would become a broad-based program of constitutional reform. The Warren Court saw the Bill of Rights and the Civil War amendments as the embodiment of the nation's highest ideals, and it soon made them the standard for judging the established order.

In the 1950s, America was not a pretty sight. Jim Crow reigned supreme. Blacks were systematically disenfranchised and excluded from juries. State-fostered religious practices, such as school prayer, were

pervasive. Legislatures were grossly gerrymandered and malappor-
tioned. McCarthyism stifled dissent, and the jurisdiction of the censor
over matters deemed obscene or libelous had no constitutional limits.
The heavy hand of the criminal law threatened those who publicly provided information and advice about contraceptives, imperiling the most
intimate of human relationships and exposing women to the unique bur-
dens of unwanted pregnancies. The states had a virtually free hand in
the administration of criminal justice. Trials often proceeded without
counsel or jury. Convictions were allowed to stand even when they
turned on illegally seized evidence or on statements extracted from the
accused by coercion. There were no rules limiting the imposition of the
death penalty. These features of the criminal justice system victimized
the poor and disadvantaged. So too did the welfare system, which was
administered in an arbitrary and oppressive manner. The capacity of the
poor to participate in civic activities was also limited by the imposition
of poll taxes, court filing fees, and the like. It was precisely these evils
that the Warren Court, at the peak of its powers, so readily and ably
took on.

Of course the Warren Court did not act in a political or social vacuum.
It drew on broad-based protests and demonstrations by the civil rights
and welfare rights movements. At critical junctures it looked to the executive and legislative branches for support. The dual school system of
Jim Crow could not have been dismantled without the troops in Little
Rock, the Civil Rights Act of 1964, the interventions of the Department
of Justice and the Department of Health, Education, and Welfare, the
lawsuits of the NAACP Legal Defense Fund, or the countless Black citizens who dared to become plaintiffs or, just as important, dared to break
the color line at school or work or to march in defense of their rights.
Without the involvement of all of these institutions and individuals, the
1960s would not have been what they became, and the world that emerged
from that period would look very different. Yet it is also true that the
Warren Court spurred the great changes of this period, and inspired and
protected those who sought to implement them.

A constitutional program so daring and so bold was, of course, the work of many minds. It is customary to use the Chief Justice's name when referring to a period of Supreme Court history. In Warren's case, this practice seems especially appropriate. Earl Warren was a man of dignity and vision, in every respect a leader, who discharged his duties (even the most trivial, like admitting new members to the bar) with grace and cheerfulness. He presided in a way that filled the courtroom with a glow. Bernard Schwartz called Warren "Super Chief," and the title seemed apt. Yet the work of the Court Warren led and the revolution it effectuated in our understanding of the Constitution drew on the talents and ideas of all those who found themselves entrusted with the judicial power at that unusual moment in history.

Justice Brennan's contribution to this ensemble was singular. He was fully devoted to the values we identify with the Warren Court—equality, procedural fairness, freedom of speech, and religious liberty—and was fully prepared to act on them. Beyond that, he was the one who was primarily assigned the task of speaking for the Court. It was Brennan who by and large formulated the principles, analyzed the precedents, and chose the words that forged ideals into law. Like all master craftsmen, he left his imprint on the finished product.

In the great constitutional cases of the day, Warren and Brennan were usually on the same side. They served together for thirteen Terms and agreed in 89 percent of the more than 1,400 cases they decided. Indeed, with the possible exception of obscenity regulation, it is hard to think of any matter of importance on which they differed. As Chief Justice, Warren was responsible for assigning the task of speaking for the Court when, as usually happened, his position prevailed. Sometimes, as in *Reynolds v. Sims* and *Miranda v. Arizona*, where the issue was especially close to his heart, or where he felt the need for the imprimatur of his office, Warren wrote the opinion. *Reynolds* set the "one-person, one-vote" standard in legislative apportionment cases; *Miranda* required the police to inform suspects of their right to counsel. In general, however, the Chief Justice turned to Justice Brennan to write the opinion for the majority.

In part, this practice reflected the unusual personal tie that developed between Warren and Brennan. The Chief—as Brennan always called him, even in face-to-face conversation—visited Brennan's chambers frequently. Each visit was an important occasion for the chambers as a whole and for Justice Brennan in particular. One could see at a glance the admiration and affection that each felt for the other. The relationship between Earl Warren and William Brennan was one of the most extraordinary relationships between two judges that the law has ever known.

More than personal sentiment was involved in turning to Brennan; Warren could be certain that the task of writing the opinion for the Court was in the hands of someone who shared both his underlying values and his commitment to the Court as an institution. Assigning an opinion is always an expression of trust, and Warren wholly trusted Brennan to formulate and express the Court's position in a way that would strengthen the Court in the eyes of both the public and the profession, and thus enhance its capacity to do its great work. Brennan was, in the highest and best sense of the word, a statesman: not a person who tempers principle with prudence, but one who is capable of grasping a multiplicity of conflicting principles, some of which relate to the well-being of the institution. In addition, he recognized that a judge's duty is not just to speak the law, but to see to it that it becomes an actuality—to make sure, in the words of *Cooper v. Aaron,* that the law becomes "a living truth."

Brennan could be trusted to choose his words in a way that would minimize disagreement among the Justices, both to avoid the silly squabbles that can interfere with the smooth functioning of a collegial institution and to broaden the agreement and thus strengthen the force of each ruling. Only five votes are needed for a decision to become law, but the larger the majority and the broader the consensus, the stronger its claim of authority. Brennan could also be trusted to respect the traditions of the bar and to pay homage to the principle of stare decisis. He always tried to build from within. Sometimes that was not possible because the break with the past was too great. Yet even then, Brennan's inclination, always rooted in a concern for the Court's authority, was to minimize disruption, to find, if at all possible, the narrow path through the precedents. Brennan also understood that reforms as bold as those the Court was trying to effectuate required coordination, not separation, of powers, and so worked to avoid gratuitous confrontations with the other branches. In fact, as is evident from Justice Brennan's opinion in *Katzenbach v. Morgan*, which affirmed a broad conception of congressional power under Section 5 of the Fourteenth Amendment, every effort was made to invite the other branches of government to collaborate on the program of constitutional reform in which the Court was engaged.

Aside from a proper respect for institutional needs, a successful opinion requires a mastery of legal craft. This, too, Warren found in Brennan. Justice Brennan was as much a lawyer as he was a statesman. Law is a blend of the theoretical and the technical, and though others may have been as gifted as Brennan in the formulation of a theoretical principle, no one in the ruling coalition—certainly not before Fortas's appointment—had either the patience or the natural ability to master the technical detail of the law in the way that Brennan did. Everyone at the Court, law clerk and Justice alike, admired Brennan's command of vast bodies of learning, ancient and modern. He knew the cases and the statutes and how they interacted; he also understood how the legal system worked and how it might be made to work better. Among the majority, he was the lawyer's judge.

Even Brennan's most theoretically ambitious opinions, such as *New York Times Co. v. Sullivan*, bear the lawyer's mark. In that case, Justice Brennan spoke in broad terms of a national commitment to public debate that is "uninhibited, robust, and wide-open," and as a result, his opinion has been justly celebrated for reformulating, in a fresh and original way, the theory of free speech associated with the work of Alexander Meiklejohn. Meiklejohn, then in his nineties, saw Brennan's opinion in *New York Times Co. v. Sullivan* as "an occasion for dancing in the streets." Of even greater importance to lawyers and judges (Meiklejohn was, after all, a political theorist) was Brennan's careful analysis of the common law of libel and his deft reformulation of doctrine—the announcement of the "actual malice" requirement—to create a rule that could be applied and that would also strike a just accommodation between reputational interests and democratic values. Today *New York Times Co. v. Sullivan* remains a revered decision, a fountainhead of freedom precisely because it was an exercise in political philosophy made law.

In 1968, history took a new turn. In June of that year, months before the November election, but with a view as to its likely outcome, Chief Justice Warren tendered his resignation to President Johnson. Warren assumed that Johnson would choose Abe Fortas, the President's confidant, to replace him as Chief Justice. However, the Senate rejected this plan and Fortas's nomination for the Chief Justiceship was withdrawn. As a result, following the 1968 election, Nixon, capitalizing on Earl Warren's resignation, appointed Warren Burger as Chief Justice. The next year, Justice Fortas was forced to resign from the Court altogether owing to newly revealed financial improprieties. Soon thereafter, John Harlan and Hugo Black each retired. Thus, in the span of four years, President Nixon, no friend of the Warren Court, was able to make three Supreme Court appointments in addition to that of Burger. In time, one of those appointees, Harry Blackmun, developed a view of the Constitution aligned with the Warren Court's precepts. But the other new Associate Justices, Lewis Powell and William Rehnquist, were of a different character. There were differences between the views of Powell and Rehnquist, but the views of both were sharply at odds with the jurisprudence that reigned in the 1960s.

The final dissolution of the majority that had given life to the Warren Court came with the resignation of Douglas in 1975 and his replacement, by President Gerald Ford, with John Paul Stevens. The balance of power had shifted decisively and was then locked in place by two accidents of history: Jimmy Carter, the President from 1976 to 1980, made no appointments (a distinction shared with no other President who completed a full term), while Ronald Reagan, his successor, made three: Antonin Scalia (to fill the vacancy created by Burger's resignation), Sandra Day O'Connor (to replace Stewart), and Anthony Kennedy (to replace

Powell). In 1986, at the same time he appointed Scalia, President Reagan elevated Rehnquist to the Chief Justiceship. This change, however, only conformed outward appearances to the inner reality. For much of the 1970s and early 1980s Rehnquist had led the Court, building the necessary coalitions, setting the agenda of the governing majority, and formulating the methods of revision. Even during Burger's years it was the Rehnquist Court.

These changes ushered in a new phase of Supreme Court history, and Justice Brennan found himself working in a radically different environment. He could still turn to allies like Thurgood Marshall and, in time, Harry Blackmun, and now and then John Paul Stevens, for support, but for the most part the going was rough. No longer a dominant figure in the ruling coalition, Brennan became part of the opposition, pitted against a majority that was driven by a vision of American law and life that saw the Warren Court's achievements as so many mistakes to be limited, corrected, even eradicated.

Retrenchment came in school desegregation. *Brown*, of course, was not overruled, but from the mid-1970s on it was drained of much of its generative power. The Court ruled that school systems containing many all-black and all-white schools were constitutionally acceptable. For the new majority, *Brown* condemned only the use of racial criteria as an official method of school assignment, not the inequalities resulting from the actual separation of the races. As a result, the Court allowed school boards to assign students to schools on the basis of neighborhoods, even when the neighborhoods were themselves racially segregated. In the 1974 ruling in *Milliken v. Bradley* so thoroughly denounced by Thurgood Marshall, the new majority also effectively insulated overwhelmingly white suburban communities from the reach of court orders aimed at desegregating inner-city schools. School boards remain obliged to correct for vestiges of past practices, such as blatant racial gerrymandering of school attendance districts, but the Court shifted the emphasis and articulated a limited vision of the obligation to desegregate that *Brown* had imposed.

Even outside the school desegregation context, the Warren Court's egalitarianism was curbed. In *Moose Lodge No. 107 v. Irvis*, which upheld the issuance of a state liquor license to a club that openly discriminated on the basis of race, the constitutional ban on discrimination was confined to "state action" narrowly understood. At roughly the same time, the Court ruled in *Washington v. Davis* that, to establish a denial of equal protection under the Constitution, it would not be enough to show that the state action disproportionately disadvantaged minorities; petitioners would also have to show that the state had intended this effect. Likewise, in *San Antonio Independent School District v. Rodriguez*, the Court effectively removed the poor from the scope of the Equal Protection Clause, leaving the War on Poverty more vulnerable than ever to the vicissitudes of politics. In the same case, the Court also declared that education was not a fundamental right, thereby bringing to a halt the process that gained prominence in the 1960s of enumerating those rights that warranted special judicial solicitude. Moreover, as the commitment to ensuring the equality of the size of electoral districts waned, the Court became more and more tolerant of departures from the "one person, one vote" standard.

The new majority also chiseled fresh cracks into the wall between church and state, allowing the government to engage in practices that would previously have been unthinkable, like maintaining a public Christmas crèche. Lacking their predecessors' steely tolerance for protest, the new majority also upheld laws denying political activists the opportunity to address citizens gathered at popular locations such as shopping centers. It even sustained a municipal regulation barring political candidates from posting broadsides on utility poles. Perversely, the Court increasingly used the First Amendment to strike down laws limiting the influence of wealth in political elections and referendums, even though those measures were aimed at preserving the vitality of democratic politics by preventing the wealthy from drowning out the voices of the less affluent. In these cases and others, the new majority seemed to have confused the protection of speech with the protection of property.

In the criminal context, the new majority lifted the ban on the application of the death penalty, which had its roots in the late 1960s and formally took effect in the early 1970s. Between 1976 and 1990, when Brennan retired, more than 140 persons convicted of crimes were put to death. Rehnquist, both as a Justice and in his role as head of the Judicial Conference of the United States after becoming Chief Justice, instituted procedural changes that expedited and facilitated this process. In the same period, the Court shifted the balance of advantage in the criminal process, relaxing hard-won restrictions on the investigatory activities of the police, especially rules excluding illegally seized evidence from trial.

During the 1960s the Warren Court had opened the doors of the federal trial courts for the issuance of writs of habeas corpus allowing federal judges to examine state court convictions, and for the issuance of injunctions halting state criminal proceedings. Those decisions helped ensure that state criminal courts adhered to minimum standards of fairness and that criminal prosecutions would not be used for improper purposes, such as the harassment of political activists. In the 1970s and 1980s, though, those doors were closed. *Fay v. Noia* and *Dombrowski v. Pfister*, opinions by Brennan that helped make federal courts the primary forum for protecting federal rights, were deprived of all operative significance. A similar fate befell *Goldberg v. Kelly*, also written by Brennan, which had extended the due process revolution of the 1960s from the criminal to the civil domain. Determined to confine *Goldberg v. Kelly* to its narrowest compass, the new majority allowed the government to inflict grievous suffering on individuals, such as denying disability benefits and terminating parental rights, without providing even the most elementary forms of due process.

Law moves unevenly, and even after Warren stepped down there were a few bright moments. During Brennan's tenure, the most significant were *Roe v. Wade*, the 1973 decision creating a right to abortion, and *Regents of the University of California v. Bakke*, the 1978 decision indicating, in theory, that certain preferential treatment programs for minorities were permissible. No one should belittle those achievements, or any other that might come to mind, but they cannot be taken as representative of the judicial era of which they are a part. *Roe v. Wade* and *Bakke* did not insert new premises into the law, but rather built on understandings of an earlier time. These decisions were hard-fought victories that sharply divided the Court, and to this day they survive by the narrowest of margins. At present, they define the outer limits of the law, without generative power of their own.

Living through the 1970s and 1980s was not easy for Justice Brennan. It tested him, but also brought many of his strengths to the fore. Values that he shared with others on the Court in the 1960s became distinguishing features of the Justice in the next two decades, and then became a source of his identity and greatness. These values—and his willingness to act on them—were largely responsible for the outpouring of admiration and affection at the time of his retirement and the eagerness of many to send him off as a national hero. In celebrating him, people were in part celebrating the liberal tradition that he helped to create and defend and that now seemed increasingly imperiled. In some instances, Brennan's understanding of the Constitution evolved in the 1970s and 1980s, as when, in obscenity cases, he moved toward the unqualified commitment to free speech long identified with Justices Black and Douglas. For the most part, however, these years were for Brennan a period devoted to defending the Warren Court's earlier achievements.

In the 1970s and 1980s, Brennan's role changed from spokesperson to critic of the prevailing majority, and the result was a profusion of dissents. One enterprising law clerk calculated that over his career Justice Brennan wrote dissenting opinions in 2,347 cases, and most of them were written during the 1970s and 1980s. Some 1,517 were in death penalty cases, and a great number of these were formulaic dissents from denials of certiorari, jointly issued with Thurgood Marshall, reaffirming their view that the death penalty was unconstitutional. But even subtracting these, the number of dissenting opinions remains impressive: 830. In his last Term on the bench, the Justice wrote full dissenting opinions in twenty-three cases. By contrast, during the 1965 Term in which I clerked for Brennan, he wrote a dissenting opinion in only one case, *United States v. Guest*, and it is not even clear whether that opinion should be regarded as a dissent. As commentators immediately realized, though Brennan's opinion in that case was labeled a dissent, it set forth a view of congressional authority that, when read in conjunction with Justice Tom Clark's separate concurrence, had the support of a majority of five Justices. Along with *Kat{zenbach v. Morgan*, the Justice's opinion in *Guest* helped provide the constitutional foundation for the Civil Rights Act of 1968 and its ban on housing discrimination and racially motivated violence, even when committed by private actors.

In time, the number of Justice Brennan's dissents exceeded those of the first Justice Harlan and of Justice Holmes, each of whom is sometimes referred to as "the Great Dissenter." Over their careers, Harlan wrote 134 dissents and Holmes 81, numbers that seem trivial in comparison with the number of Brennan's dissents—2,347, or if the formulaic dissents of certiorari in death penalty cases are subtracted, 830. Perhaps, as one of his former law clerks announced, in a jocular mood, at a reunion of law clerks, Brennan should be called "the Greatest Dissenter."

It would be a mistake, however, to view Justice Brennan, even during this second phase of his career on the Court, as we view either Holmes or Harlan. Holmes and Harlan were both loners. Holmes, in particular, held a philosophical outlook that supremely suited him to play the role of lone dissenter. He viewed history, and even the actions of his brethren, as a detached spectator might. So even when Holmes raised his voice in protest, as he did in *Lochner v. New York*, invalidating a New York statute setting maximum hours for bakery workers, or *Abrams v. United States*, upholding the criminal conviction of antiwar critics, he did so with indifference as to whether he had convinced his colleagues or obtained their votes. Holmes spoke to the future. His intent was to speak his mind and let the chips fall wherever they might.

Justice Brennan, by contrast, was never, but never, a loner or a detached spectator. He was always thoroughly engaged with his colleagues, passionately working to build a majority that could shape the

course of the law. In the late 1950s and 1960s he built the majorities responsible for the Warren Court's revolution; in the 1970s and 1980s he
tried to build majorities to stanch the counterrevolution. Brennan's dissents spoke not to the future but to his colleagues. More often than not,
they read like majority opinions that fell just short of a fifth vote. In one
notable instance involving congressional power under the Commerce
Clause, he managed to sway one member of the initial majority to his
view, thereby transforming the position he had articulated in his *National League of Cities v. Usery* dissent into the law of the land.

Indeed, Brennan never saw his dissents as being at the core of his mission. At law clerk dinners during the 1970s and 1980s he would wryly
announce the tally of his dissents to the assembled, and we would cheer
his continued resistance. It was obvious, though, that the Justice's true
source of pleasure and pride were those cases in which he somehow—
miraculously, I think—formed a majority that held the line. In such
cases, Chief Justice Rehnquist was usually on the other side, and as a
result, Brennan would act as shadow chief, often assigning himself the
task of speaking for the odd coalition that he managed to put together to
preserve a fragment of the Warren Court's legacy.

In 1982, the Justice spoke for the Court, striking down a Texas statute
barring from public schools children who had not been legally admitted
to the United States, on the theory that the statute created "the specter
of a permanent caste of undocumented resident aliens." In 1989, Brennan
spoke for the Court in protecting flag burning as a form of protest, de-
claring: "If there is a bedrock principle underlying the First Amendment,
it is that the government may not prohibit the expression of an idea
simply because society finds the idea itself offensive or disagreeable."
Viewed from this perspective, it was entirely fitting, that on his last day
on the Court, he announced a majority opinion upholding a Federal
Communications Commission policy born of another era that built on
Bakke and favored minority interests in awarding broadcasting licenses.
Just three weeks later Justice Brennan suffered the stroke that led to his
decision to retire.

Brennan was always thoroughly devoted to the Court as an institution. In the Warren Court era his devotion accounted for his role as spokesman for the governing coalition and for the distinctive nature of his opinions. He took no pleasure in speaking alone, as he might have in a separate concurrence. His first priority was to have the Court speak authoritatively, and his second was to produce an opinion that would strengthen the effectiveness of the Court. He strove to avoid making gestures that would dissolve or splinter the majority, infuriate those on the other side of the bench, or spark political dynamics that might undermine the ability of the Court to achieve all that it might. During the second part of his tenure on the Court, these same sentiments shaped his strategy of resistance. Dissent was always a possibility, but his first priority was to have the Court speak to the issue in an authoritative manner, simply because he continued to believe that the Court and what it said mattered. He remained committed to working through the institution, not to propounding his own views, speaking his mind, or otherwise indulging himself. Dissent was a reluctant last resort—almost an acknowledgment of failure.

At the time of his retirement, the legacy of the Warren Court seemed more imperiled than ever. Justice Brennan had left a written legacy in the form of opinions that will long exert a force on the course of the law. Indeed, the pages of the United States Reports are filled with his writings, both dissents and majority opinions. Near the end of Brennan's tenure, another of his law clerks surveyed the leading casebooks on constitutional law and reported that Brennan had written more of the so-called principal cases featured in those books than any other Justice in the history of the Supreme Court. His opinions define the field within which the Court operates; for some Justices they act as constraints, for others as resources; and as David Souter, Brennan's successor, said in a eulogy at Brennan's funeral, for some Justices they might even serve as inspiration. Brennan's writings live on, but they cannot fill the void created by the loss of the personal qualities that he brought to the Justices' deliberations.

During the term I worked for the Justice, the Court held its conferences on Friday. Later that day, or more commonly on Saturday, when

Brennan regularly had lunch with his clerks, he would describe what transpired at conference, or at least what he thought we should know. He also provided insights into some of the Court's inner workings during annual dinners with his clerks in the late 1960s and early 1970s. At that time, the number of former clerks was small enough that we could sit around a table upstairs at the Occidental Grill. Those were also the days—before the publication of *The Brethren*—when a Justice could assume that law clerks could be trusted with a confidence. Justice Brennan was not a man for gossip or small talk about his colleagues (though his interest in the personal lives of his clerks was boundless—he treated us like members of his family). He saw himself as a teacher, supplementing and enriching what we might have learned in the classroom, and he believed that understanding the sometimes intense dynamics among the Justices was a crucial part of our education, especially if, as he hoped, we would go on to become teachers. He wanted us, and our students, to know how law was truly made. Although his role in the deliberations was not the principal subject of these conversations, we could easily see how the personal qualities that drew us to the man—the quickness and clarity of his mind, the warmth of his personality, the energy that he brought to argument, his sensitivity to the views of others—must have influenced what happened in the Conference Room. Justice Brennan always had more than one vote. Who could possibly resist him when he grabbed you by the elbow, or put his arm around your shoulder, and began, "Look, pal . . ."?

The Justice's retirement, soon followed by Marshall's, compounded the disaffection with the Court that then pervaded the academy and large sections of the profession. The Court was increasingly seen as an alien and hostile institution, less devoted to actualizing national ideals than to protecting the established order and belittling those who challenged it. This perception contributed to the rise of the Critical Legal Studies movement in the late 1970s and to the nihilism it propagated with the proclamation that "law is politics." At the moment of Justice Brennan's retirement, disaffection with the Court was at a peak, and his departure only nourished it. In the more than twenty-five years that have passed since then, many developments have modulated this sentiment, most notably the Supreme Court appointments by Presidents Bill Clinton and Barack Obama, and Justice Anthony Kennedy's evolving positions on some social issues. Still, many in the academy and the profession, me included, remain disaffected by much of the work of the Court, and sometimes are on the edge of agreeing that law is, indeed, just politics.

Anyone who studied at Harvard in the early 1960s, as I did, knew that the Warren Court had its critics. A number of the Harvard faculty had criticized the Court in terms most emphatic; *Brown* itself was denounced in a speech delivered under the auspices of Harvard's prestigious Holmes lectures. Brennan's response to these attacks expressed itself in many ways, one quite trivial: the Justice decided to end his practice of hiring his clerks, as a matter of course, from Harvard, his alma mater. In fact, on the final day of my clerkship, I received a poem entitled "Ode to My Last Harvard Clerk," written in the voice of Justice Brennan, by Carey Parker, a friend working for another Justice. In time, Justice Brennan's anger toward Harvard would abate. But even at the peak of the tensions it was understood that Harvard, and the other critics of the Warren Court, did not speak for the profession as a whole, and even less so for the young, who saw *Brown* and the Supreme Court's other achievements as an inspiration, the very reason to become lawyers.

The Supreme Court's decisions of the past forty years largely consist of a systematic and comprehensive attack by a powerful bloc, far too often a majority, on the ideals forged into law by the Warren Court. Even when a coalition opposed to the counterrevolution was able to win the day, it did so by the narrowest of margins, and its decisions usually lacked the vision that infused *Brown* and that so characterized the work of Justice Brennan. The Court has been fractured, unable to engender the loyalty of the young and perhaps even the bar in general. Indeed, it is sometimes difficult to see or present the body of learning known as constitutional law as worthy of respect and admiration. It is also difficult to know how the Court might continue to play its historic function in the republic: how can it speak authoritatively and effectively to the issues that divide us if the Justices themselves are so divided and the bar feels so alienated from it? To some, this loss of authority might not seem so tragic, given the overall direction of the Court's decisions. At the same time, I wonder whether such a view is inappropriately shortsighted, seeing only what is, without regard to what was and what might be. Given all that the institution once accomplished, and still might, there is reason to believe in the Court and the redemptive possibilities of law.

In musing on this quandary, my mind often turns to Justice Brennan. While the Justice represents many things for me, probably none is more important than his attachment to the Court as an institution. It unifies the two phases of his career and accounts for the unusual role that he created for himself during his last twenty years on the bench, even as he saw so much of the judicial world he created and so much that he believed in dismantled and destroyed. During all those years, Justice Brennan served cheerfully and determinedly, always with an unqualified devotion to the Court. I wonder whether those, like myself, who wish to honor him and the extraordinary age of American law that he helped bring into being might not look to him as an exemplar and an inspiration. He resisted, tenaciously, and yet kept the faith—why can't we?

John Doar in Jackson, Mississippi, on June 15, 1963, after the funeral of Medgar Evers.

3

John
Doar

To Stand for What Is Right

On May 17, 1954, the day the Supreme Court announced its decision in *Brown v. Board of Education*, a new chapter began in the history of the nation. The Court condemned the racial caste system that had long characterized American society, and in so doing initiated a process that would uproot deeply entrenched institutions and practices. In time, this process of change proved so profound and so sweeping that many have called it a civil rights revolution, though we should remember that it was a most unusual, almost paradoxical revolution: a revolution by and through the law.

The Supreme Court had called for the end of Jim Crow and then placed the task of implementing its edict on the lower federal courts. As part of the plan, federal judges throughout the South were charged with eradicating the traditional dual school system, ensuring the right to vote, and dismantling the vast network of practices that kept Blacks as second-class citizens. New statutes, most notably the Civil Rights Act of 1964 and the Voting Rights Act of 1965, reinforced these court victories and gave the principles that emerged from them new force. In some instances, Congress had to invent wholly new procedures to put those principles into practice.

Countless citizens stepped forward to demand an end to Jim Crow. Their action was nonviolent, and it took many different forms—boycotts, freedom rides, sit-ins, voter registration campaigns, and marches. The law played a crucial role in all these activities. The protesters invoked the authority of the Supreme Court and insisted that the rights conferred by the Constitution be respected and, if need be, new judicial decisions rendered and statutes enacted for that purpose. The law was also forged into a shield to protect those who sought radical change. State convictions of those who "sat in" were overturned by the Supreme Court, and the lower federal courts were, now and then, called on to protect those who marched or helped others register to vote.

On a number of occasions the armed forces of the nation were deployed, as in the Little Rock school desegregation crisis of 1957 and the effort in 1962 to register James Meredith as a student at Ole Miss. Even then, law was central. The military was used to ensure the implementation of court orders and, by endowing law with the force of arms, helped bring the old order to an end.

As these tumultuous developments began to unfold, the lawyers of the nation were summoned to the temple of justice. They were asked for all the goodness they possessed to help deliver on the Constitution's promise of equality. Thanks to a Princeton connection, John Doar received his call in the spring of 1960, during the waning days of the presidency of Dwight Eisenhower, when he was asked to serve as First Assistant to Harold Tyler, Assistant Attorney General in charge of the Civil Rights Division. Doar left his family's law firm in New Richmond, Wisconsin, and headed east. He arrived in Washington, D.C., on July 4, 1960.

The presidential election that November brought a Democrat, John Kennedy, to the White House, who appointed his brother, Robert Kennedy, as Attorney General. In turn, Robert Kennedy selected Burke Marshall, a highly respected Washington lawyer, to head the Civil Rights

Division. Marshall saw something special in Doar and asked him to stay on as his First Assistant. Marshall, deeply shaken by the assassination of President Kennedy in November 1963, remained on the job for a little more than a year. When he stepped down, Lyndon Johnson promoted John Doar to serve as Assistant Attorney General in charge of the Division. John served in that capacity until the end of 1967 and during his tenure would answer to two very different Attorney Generals, Nicholas Katzenbach and Ramsey Clark. John never made much of his formal titles. He always introduced himself as an attorney in the Department of Justice.

John fully appreciated the importance of the private bar and its representation of individuals who claimed their rights had been denied. He believed that these efforts accounted for much of the dynamic quality of American law. Yet John sharply differentiated the responsibilities of a lawyer in the Department of Justice from those of a lawyer representing an aggrieved individual, and he was always mindful of the special responsibilities he shouldered because he represented the United States.

The United States is the most unusual of clients, in part because it has resources and power possessed by no other. Sometimes, though, the power seems greater to an outsider than it is. Working for John in 1966 and 1967, I marveled at the paucity of lawyers then in the Civil Rights Division—only about forty. In the summer of 1960, when John began his career with the Division, the number of lawyers was even fewer—only about twenty, some with scant experience.

Still, John was acutely aware of the unique power of the United States, both because of its vast financial and material resources and its special prerogatives, including its capacity to initiate criminal prosecutions or to seek injunctions to halt ongoing state proceedings. John understood that when he spoke he was speaking for the nation, and thus he went about his work with an added sense of responsibility and circumspection.

John also understood that because he represented the United States his obligation to justice was absolute and unqualified. He embraced with remarkable tenacity the familiar maxim, "The United States wins when justice is done." Of course, the requirements of justice do not always reveal themselves. John knew that and was fully aware of the uncertainties of the law.

John's way of discovering the meaning of justice was not that of Plato. He had no taste for abstract reflection. Instead he focused on a specific, concrete situation and sought to find the principles of justice immanent in it. John emphasized the facts and the importance of getting them right, absolutely right. "Facts, facts, facts" was his mantra.

In truth, John worried about the law as much as he did about the facts. He endlessly deliberated about the law with his staff, usually in his large corner office, sometimes with Burke Marshall on the phone, long after Burke had left the Department. Now and then I would get a call from John in the middle of the night to go over some point of law about which he felt uneasy.

Not only was John's search for justice relentless, it was also sometimes remorseless, when, for example, he firmly rejected, because it was not quite right, a brief or a complaint that the staff had worked on for days and days. No mistake about it—these rejections stung. But we soon got over our bruised feelings, and when we did, we marveled at John's exactitude and respected him for it. I even enjoyed the teasing arising from my gaffes, teasing that, I must admit, sometimes lasted for years.

John had a passion for what might properly be called legwork. The Division was based in Washington, but John insisted that the staff spend a great deal of time in those communities where rights were being violated and where the Constitution remained unenforced. He wanted the Division's lawyers to see, firsthand, the Jim Crow system at work. He also wanted them to develop good working relationships with local officials, including the administrative offices of the federal courts who might someday be needed to keep their offices open after hours for a late filing.

For these reasons, John reorganized the Division and distributed its lawyers largely along geographic lines. Most of the forty-some attorneys in the Division in the mid-1960s were assigned to the Southeast and Southwest Sections. Lawyers in the Southeast Section focused on Georgia and Alabama (although Florida and South Carolina were also within their purview); those in the Southwest Section were responsible for Mississippi and Louisiana. A small handful of lawyers covered the rest of the country.

John himself was always in the field, even when he was Assistant Attorney General. Sometimes, he spent as many as two hundred days a year on the road, gathering facts, getting to know local communities under stress, and developing working relationships with local officials and leaders of the Civil Rights Movement. John was always on the go and in that limited sense, restless. At one moment, he might be in Montgomery, then in Mobile, on to Jackson, then to New Orleans, back to Biloxi, and finally Houston, before heading back to Washington.

The burden of all this travel on his family was enormous. John was away from Washington when his second son was born, and thanks to the pressure of work his third son remained unnamed for six weeks. He was eventually named Burke. John loved his family deeply, but he always remained disciplined and focused on his work. He was governed not by a rigid understanding of the duties of office, but rather by the need he felt to see that justice was done. Even when he was in town, John worked well into the night and was the last to leave the office.

I began to work for John on the Thursday before Labor Day in the summer of 1966. On Friday he walked into my office and invited me to travel with him over the weekend to Montgomery, Alabama. Although the prospect of explaining to my family how I might be spending the Labor Day weekend was terrifying, I immediately said yes, and off we went. We eventually made our way to the chambers of Judge Frank Johnson.

What happened then was remarkable; as far as I could tell, it had no precedent in anything that I had been taught about the Federal Rules of

Civil Procedure. John and Judge Johnson had a wide-ranging discussion about the pace of school desegregation throughout Alabama and what might be done to accelerate it. I sat by quietly, struck by the rapport between the two men and the authority that John conveyed, not just because he spoke for the nation, but also and perhaps more important, because of his devotion to justice.

During the mid-1960s, Judge Johnson began the practice—also not contemplated by the Federal Rules—of issuing on his own accord orders that in effect pushed the United States, represented by the Department of Justice, to intervene in civil rights cases pending before him. The United States was ordered to participate in these cases as an amicus, but with almost all the rights of a party. This novel procedure, which I believe should be seen as a tribute to John, was soon adopted by other trial judges in the region.

The high regard that Judge Johnson had for John was shared by the leading figures on the Court of Appeals for the Fifth Circuit, whose jurisdiction then embraced all of the Deep South. In 1967, I carried John's briefcase to the oral argument that was to be held in Jacksonville, Florida, before the Fifth Circuit sitting en banc—a startling spectacle, all fifteen judges, arrayed in two tiers. The Court of Appeals was reviewing the decision of a panel of judges penned by Judge John Minor Wisdom, that had established a uniform school desegregation plan for the entire Circuit.

At argument, James Nabrit of the NAACP Legal Defense Fund was pressed by one of the judges: "What are you asking for?" Nabrit's answer consisted of a lawyerly but complicated analysis of the distinction between "integration" and "desegregation" and the precise role numerical goals should play in determining whether the constitutional duty had been satisfied. When John rose, he was asked the same question— "What are you asking for?"—but his answer transcended the controversies that Nabrit's nuanced response had provoked. Borrowing a line from Judge Wisdom's panel opinion, later to appear in an opinion by Justice Brennan, John declared that "the government wants not white schools and not schools for Negro children—but just plain schools." When John spoke, the judges listened, and did so with an intensity that was attributable to their respect for John's integrity and sense of fairness.

The authority that John and the Division exercised was not to everyone's liking. The defendants grumbled, of course. More surprisingly, so did some of the NAACP lawyers. They resented John's refusal to share the Department's briefs with them before filing, even though they were also participants in the case and presumably on the same side. Similar frustrations were sometimes felt by civil rights activists when they made demands on John that he felt he could not, as a matter of principle, honor. They repeatedly sought police protection, but John denied those requests and explained that providing safety was the responsibility of the states. This hardly reassured civil rights activists who saw the states in which they were working, above all Alabama and Mississippi, as being at war with *Brown* and all that it stood for. Who would police the police, they wondered? Who would protect them from an unruly mob when the local police wouldn't?

The anger and resentment that the Civil Rights Movement sometimes felt toward the Division has lessened, sometimes even been ignored, in recent years. The dynamics that led to the belated rapprochement are fully understandable—tempers have cooled, and the differences between the protagonists have been dwarfed by what they, acting in their own way, have achieved. Still, ignoring the tensions between the Division and the Civil Rights Movement not only distorts the historical record; it also obscures one of John's commanding qualities—his courage. John always stood tall and straight, unwilling to bend to the passions of the day, no matter where his personal sympathies lay, and this remarkable resolve stemmed from his sense of rectitude.

There were many tests of John's courage during his days at the Civil Rights Division. The most famous, of near biblical proportions, occurred in Jackson, Mississippi, on June 15, 1963, following the funeral of Medgar Evers. On that day a line of white police officers with drawn weapons, stood facing a large group of Blacks, estimated to be in the hundreds, who had just left Evers's funeral, burdened by their grief and the heat. Evers, the field secretary of the NAACP, had been murdered in front of his home only days before. The crowd coming from the funeral had turned angry and demanded that his killer be found.

As the crowd advanced, John, then only forty-two years old, wearing a white shirt and tie, sleeves partly rolled up, stepped from behind the police line and placed himself in the space of about fifty feet between the police and those coming from the funeral. He faced the insistent crowd, raised his arms almost to the height of his shoulders, and with open hands gestured to the crowd in a way that urged them to stop advancing. At the crucial moment, as tension mounted, John captured the essence of his being and made clear the source of his courage: "My name is John Doar—D-O-A-R. I am from the Department of Justice, and as anybody around here knows, I stand for what is right. Medgar Evers would not want it this way." The angry crowd melted and began to disperse.

Fate was not always so kind. Violence sometimes erupted, and when it did, death took its toll. Such tragedies were not attributable to a personal failing of John's as much as they were a consequence of the character of our federalism—respected by John, but decried by activists—that looked primarily to the states, not to the federal government, for the enforcement of criminal law. One of the most painful incidents of violence—and the subject of the movie *Mississippi Burning*—involved the murder of three civil rights workers in June 1964, at the outset of Freedom Summer.

Freedom Summer was a program spearheaded by the Student Non-violent Coordinating Committee (SNCC) and the Congress for Racial Equality (CORE) to bring many hundreds of volunteers to Mississippi from all parts of the United States. They were to help in the drive to register Blacks to vote. On the afternoon of June 21, 1964, three young CORE activists—James Chaney from Mississippi, and Mickey Schwerner and Andrew Goodman from New York—were arrested in Neshoba County, Mississippi. Earlier in the day they had investigated the burning of the Mount Zion Methodist Church, presumably by the Ku Klux Klan. At the time of their arrest they were driving back to their office in the town of Meridian in a car that belonged to CORE. They were released by the sheriff and his deputies at around 10:30 P.M.—and then they disappeared. There was no trace of them or their car. Their disappearance was widely reported and shocked the nation.

Forty-four days later, on August 4, 1964, their bodies and their car were found by FBI agents, acting on a tip from a local resident, buried near an earthen dam in the county. Some fifty to seventy-five FBI agents had been brought to Mississippi from all parts of the country to search for the three young men. Afterward, new priorities were set for the Bureau, and a new field office was opened in Mississippi. As a result of this tragedy, John later acknowledged, the Bureau "did very clearly turn a corner."

The statutes available to support a federal prosecution of the perpetrators of this crime were limited. In the spring of 1966 the Supreme Court handed down a number of decisions that enlarged the authority of Congress to enforce the Fourteenth Amendment. That authority was exercised by Congress in April 1968, just a week after the assassination of Martin Luther King, when it enacted the Civil Rights Act of 1968, containing broad provisions criminalizing race-based violence. In 1964, however, the only statutes available to the federal government to deal with such violence dated from Reconstruction days. One, Section 242, prohibited persons acting "under color of law" from depriving others of their rights under the Constitution or laws of the United States. The other statute, Section 241, made it unlawful to conspire to "injure, oppress, threaten, or intimidate any citizen in the free exercise" of their constitutional or federal rights.

Under these statutes, the government indicted eighteen—later reduced to seventeen—men, including three local law enforcement officials (a sheriff, a deputy sheriff, and a patrolman). The defendants were charged with violating Section 242 and, under the general conspiracy statute, with participating in a conspiracy to violate Section 242. Both of these offenses were punishable as misdemeanors. The defendants were also charged with violating Section 241, which by its own terms, prohibited conspiracies to interfere forcibly with the exercise of federal rights. It was punishable as a felony.

In February 1965 the federal trial judge, Harold Cox, dismissed the charges under Section 241. He also dismissed the Section 242 charges against all defendants except the three local law enforcement officials, though he allowed the government to proceed against all of the defendants on the count in the indictment that charged a conspiracy to violate Section 242—a misdemeanor. In dismissing the Section 242 charges, he denied that the persons who were not law enforcement officials were acting "under color of law." In dismissing the Section 241 charges, Cox denied that the rights the defendants were accused of violating arose under the Constitution or laws of the United States. They were rights, Cox declared, that existed before the Constitution was established.

Reflecting the urgency of the prosecution for the nation, the government took an appeal of Cox's ruling directly to the Supreme Court, bypassing the Court of Appeals. In March 1966, and as part of the line of decisions enlarging the criminal jurisdiction of the national government, the Supreme Court reversed the lower court's judgment and in doing so stressed the participation of the local law enforcement officials in the killings of the three young men. As the indictment charged, following their release at 10:30 P.M., the three civil rights workers had been arrested once again and turned over to the Klan, who then killed them and burned their car. As for the Section 242 charges, the Supreme Court held, "Private persons, jointly engaged with state officials in the prohibitive action are acting 'under color of law.'" In sustaining the Section 241 charges, the Court stressed the statute's "plain and unlimited" language and concluded that Congress had the authority to enact the statute under the Fourteenth Amendment. In upholding the applicability of Section 241, the Court focused, as it had on applying Section 242, on the involvement of the local law enforcement officers in the conspiracy.

Understanding the importance of the case for the rule of law, John personally assumed responsibility for the prosecution. He headed the investigation and tried the case. He was of course assisted by the Division lawyers, most notably by his First Assistant, Bob Owen, but John made the opening and closing arguments, examined a good number of the government's witnesses, and cross-examined some of the witnesses put on the stand by the defendants. The trial, held in Meridian, Mississippi, began on October 8, 1967, and was submitted to the jury on October 18, 1967. Two days later the jury returned a verdict that acquitted seven of the defendants, indicated its inability to reach a verdict for three, and most remarkably, convicted seven. These seven were convicted, not of murder, but as charged under Section 241 for conspiring to interfere with the exercise of federal constitutional rights. The sentences for those convicted ranged from three to ten years.

Following the trial, ending the long, grueling days in Meridian, and bringing to a head a project that had occupied him for more than three years, John returned to his desk in Washington. Soon, though, he decided that it was time to move on. He left the Division at the end of the year. In the early months of 1968, John moved to New York City to become the President of a nonprofit charged with the redevelopment of the Bedford-Stuyvesant neighborhood. While holding that position he was also appointed President of the New York City Board of Education.

Near the end of 1973, John was once again called to Washington, when the nation faced yet another test of the rule of law, this one arising from the Watergate scandal. The House Judiciary Committee had set out to determine whether there were grounds to impeach President Richard Nixon. The Chairman of that Committee, Peter Rodino, a Democrat from New Jersey, appointed John—a lifelong Republican—to head the investigation. John's Republican credentials might have helped, but it seems fair to say that Rodino was drawn primarily by the extraordinary qualities of intellect and character that John had revealed during the civil rights era.

As part of his staff for the Impeachment Inquiry, John recruited some of those who had worked with him in the Civil Rights Division, and he soon established within the ranks the same esprit de corps that prevailed under his leadership of the Division. John insisted that the staff proceed with fairness and balanced judgment, and he cultivated that ethos in countless ways—some seemingly trivial, like requiring that Nixon always be referred to as the President. Predictably, John also developed a strong working relationship with the lawyer who had been appointed by the Republican members of the Committee, the prominent Chicago lawyer Albert Jenner. In the end, Jenner joined in almost all the key recommendations that John had made to the Committee.

The task of the impeachment staff differed in one major respect from that of the Civil Rights Division. Under John's supervision, the lawyers in the Division were focused primarily on field investigations. Sometimes they were aided by FBI agents, but for the most part it was the lawyers of the Division who interviewed those who had suffered under Jim Crow, examined the records maintained by local officials, prepared witnesses, and checked whether federal court orders had been properly obeyed. In contrast, the staff of the Impeachment Inquiry did not embark on independent field investigations; instead the lawyers gathered, distilled, and synthesized information provided by others, such as the Senate Watergate Committee headed by Senator Sam Ervin, and the office of Special Prosecutor Archibald Cox.

In the course of Senator Ervin's hearings it was publicly revealed that President Nixon had secretly recorded every conversation that occurred in the Oval Office during his time in office. In April 1974, President Nixon voluntarily released to the public a transcript of some of the conversations that took place during the period under investigation. A number of individuals on John's staff, however, came to the conclusion that the transcripts released did not accurately reflect the taped conversations. The staff pressed the White House until they obtained the original recordings, and they then created a transcript of their own. The discrepancies between the "sanitized" transcript President Nixon had released and the one John's staff produced had damning consequences for the President in the court of public opinion.

The President's position continued to deteriorate over the next few months. On July 24, 1974, the Supreme Court ruled that the President was required to turn over to the Special Prosecutor various tapes and documents relating to conversations the President had with his staff after the Watergate break-in. Over the following week, the House Committee on the Judiciary voted in favor of three articles of impeachment. On August 9, 1974, President Nixon resigned, and Gerald Ford, until recently the Speaker of the House, assumed the presidency.

In this national drama the retranscription of the Nixon tapes by the Impeachment Inquiry may have been a pivotal moment. Late in his life John often spoke of it with special pride. Although in essential respects the retranscription was similar to the investigative field work of the Civil Rights Division, in truth it was an exception. The staff of the Impeachment Inquiry mostly combed through the information gathered by others or provided by the President himself to determine whether there were grounds for impeachment. Under John's supervision the staff prepared reports referred to as "Statements of Information" that were eventually to be presented to the members of the House Judiciary Committee. Crucially, these reports were not traditional "Statements of Facts," for it was the members of the Committee, as John often insisted, who were the ones to decide what the facts were. Yet the Statements of Information were constructed with the same care, the same attention to detail, and the same determined effort to be balanced and impartial that had defined the trial briefs of the Civil Rights Division.

Over a number of weeks, John personally presented the Statements of Information to the Committee. Apparently indifferent to the television cameras, he read them slowly and methodically, deliberately avoiding any inflection. His affect was that not of an inquisitor but of a dispassionate seeker of the truth. This was the same John Doar who had appeared in the courtrooms of the South. This was the same John Doar who had walked out onto a street in Jackson, Mississippi, following the funeral of Medgar Evers and, through sheer force of character, calmed an angry crowd and prevented a bloody massacre.

By the end of 1974, John had returned to New York, and until his death in November 2014, at age ninety-two, he was for the most part engaged in the private practice of law. Dorothy Landsberg, a trusted friend who long served John in his Washington days, remarked at the time of his death that John always led by example. In saying this, Dorothy spoke for all of us who had been on his staff in the Civil Rights Division or the Impeachment Inquiry, or both. We pushed ourselves in the way that he pushed himself. We measured ourselves in the way that he measured himself. We abided by the same maxims of fairness that he did. I should add, however, that John not only led, but also taught, by example, and that his lessons can guide even those who were not lucky enough to have worked for him.

John's name and his stories will serve as an inspiration to anyone who seeks justice through law. More broadly, he will remain a model for anyone who wonders how best to lead a good and noble life. Indeed, I would say of John Doar what he often said of Burke Marshall: "He was the kind of man who only comes about every 600 years." In the summer of 1960, John put aside any sensible regard for his career and began what might have seemed to be a short stint in the Department of Justice, but which in fact turned into a life-defining challenge.

History will record John Doar's many achievements, but the most significant and most enduring will be his tireless efforts to transform the near-revolutionary edict of *Brown* into a living truth. He showed the nation in vivid detail how radical change can be achieved through law and what should be expected of an attorney, maybe any attorney, but certainly one representing the United States: an unqualified and absolute devotion to justice. On May 29, 2012, President Barack Obama awarded John the Medal of Freedom, and on that occasion the President said of John, in a remarkably low-key manner, "It's fair to say that I might not be here had it not been for his work."

Burke Marshall, standing, with Attorney General Robert Kennedy on June 11, 1963, presumably dealing with the crisis arising from the action of Governor George Wallace—"standing in the schoolhouse door"—to prevent the integration of the University of Alabama.

4

Burke
Marshall

A Reluctant Hero

He loved to tease me. He knew my heart was pure, but he was amused by the excesses of reason to which I was often drawn. Burke Marshall aspired to a workable government. I, Quixote-like, wanted something more perfect—a heaven on earth. Burke understood the foolishness of my dream but always tempered his reserve with kindness and made light of our differences.

Burke began his public career as part of the Kennedy administration. The President appointed him as Assistant Attorney General in charge of the Civil Rights Division, and this appointment marked the beginning of a sea change in the civil rights policies of the federal government. Although Congress had in 1957 created the Civil Rights Division of the Department of Justice, under President Eisenhower the Division remained understaffed and relatively inactive. Eisenhower had stood by the decision in *Brown v. Board of Education* when he used federal troops, in a showdown with Arkansas governor Orval Faubus, to ensure the admission of Black students to a formerly all-white high school in Little

Rock. But the overall tone of his administration was reflected in Eisenhower's comment on *Brown* that "it is difficult through law and through force to change a man's heart."

In his 1960 campaign John Kennedy indicated he was intent on pursuing a new course in civil rights, and eventually Burke Marshall was charged with charting it. At the time of his appointment, Burke was a partner in the Washington law firm of Covington & Burling, specializing in antitrust law. Burke acknowledged at his confirmation hearing that he had no experience in civil rights litigation and was not involved with civil rights activities in any way. In fact, when he first met with Robert Kennedy, the Attorney General, he assumed he was being interviewed for the Antitrust Division. As it turns out, Burke had been recommended to head the Civil Rights Division by Byron White, then Deputy Attorney General and a fellow Yale graduate. He saw in Burke the qualities of character and intellect that would advance the cause and, at the same time, engender respect even from those otherwise bent on resisting any change.

Burke was a modest man who resisted any fanfare. As Assistant Attorney General he insisted on the changes that *Brown* decreed—the end of Jim Crow—in a quiet, determined manner. Sometimes a situation would spin out of control and violence would erupt, which had to be met with armed force. This occurred, for example, when the Department of Justice sought to implement a federal court order, issued in a suit brought by a Black student, James Meredith, requiring the integration of Ole Miss. On the night of September 30, 1962, a riot broke out on the campus of the university, resulting in two deaths and injuries to more than three hundred people. Earlier the Department of Justice had relied on U.S. Marshals—traditionally employed to serve summonses—to accompany Meredith in his effort to register. Only when that strategy failed and a riot erupted was the U.S. Army brought onto campus to restore order and implement the decree by force of arms.

Such an exercise of force was the exception. For the most part Burke achieved his purposes through the reason of the law. Burke was one of the principal architects of the bill that eventually became the Civil Rights Act of 1964. In pursuing a strategy that would eventually prove successful before the High Court, he persuaded Congress to use the Commerce Clause as the source of the federal government's authority to ban racial discrimination in places of public accommodation.

Burke also turned to the courts when necessary. In the early 1960s, Congress had only authorized the Division to bring lawsuits to protect voting rights, and under his leadership the number of such suits grew enormously. Although he confidently entrusted the day-to-day management of the Division's litigation to his First Assistant, John Doar, Burke himself participated in cases that raised novel issues and that had far-reaching consequences. In *United States v. Wood*, for example, the burden fell on Burke to identify for the Fifth Circuit—which relied heavily on his brief—the interest that the federal government had in enjoining a state criminal proceeding that was brought against John Hardy, a Student Nonviolent Coordinating Committee (SNCC) worker in Walthall County, Mississippi, for helping Blacks register to vote. When the registrar turned away elderly citizens whom he was helping, Hardy approached the clerk to see what was wrong. The clerk ordered Hardy to leave, and as he began to do so the clerk struck him on the back of the head with a pistol. Dazed and hobbled, Hardy turned to the sheriff for assistance, and when he found him, the sheriff responded by arresting Hardy for disturbing the peace.

Burke also achieved fame for resolving, through negotiation, some of the era's tensest standoffs, as he did in Birmingham, Alabama, in May 1963. After a tumultuous campaign led by Martin Luther King, he forged an agreement with the city's business and civic leaders that began the process of desegregation and ended the demonstrations that had been taking place in the city shortly before Easter. In the course of these demonstrations, which were met with fire hoses and police dogs, King was arrested and, for a short period, imprisoned; his "Letter from Birmingham Jail" almost immediately conveyed to the world the crisis that America was then facing. We were at a crossroads.

In the summer of 1963, I was in Washington, D.C. The city was abuzz with preparations for the March on Washington, to be held on August 28. My wife and I attended a meeting or two held in preparation for the March, but I was in the city for another purpose altogether. I had just finished my second year of law school and had managed to land a summer job at Covington & Burling. The work was all-consuming but, alas, dreary. I spent my days reviewing invoices for "corn syrup unmixed" to see if I could detect a violation of the Robinson-Patman Act's ban on price discrimination. It was hard for me to feign enthusiasm for my task.

One day in the last week of July, feeling discouraged, I grabbed a sandwich for lunch and ate it by myself in Lafayette Park. While reading the newspaper I came across an article describing a desegregation agreement that had ended four months of demonstrations on the Eastern Shore of Maryland. As I read on, I discovered that Burke Marshall had been largely responsible for the breakthrough. I then remembered that the memorandums in the file I had been working on that morning had all been initialed by Burke, before his departure for the government. So I managed to convince myself to persist, on the theory that "corn syrup unmixed" and all that it implied might be indispensable training for someone who hoped to one day be entrusted with the kinds of responsibilities that had been bestowed upon Burke Marshall.

I returned to Harvard in the beginning of August to work on the *Law Review*. From Cambridge I watched the March on Washington on television at a friend's house. Even at that remove I was touched by King's dream and the fervor of those present, and my sense of concern was intensified only weeks later when the Sixteenth Street Baptist Church in Birmingham was bombed and four young Black girls were killed. As the fall semester unfolded, the civil rights struggle took on even greater urgency, and I found myself uneasy with the prospect of working for a law firm. History was being made, and I wanted to be a part of it NOW.

In early November, only weeks before the assassination of President Kennedy, I flew from Boston to Washington with the wild idea of presenting myself to Burke Marshall for a job following my graduation from law school. After arriving in Washington, I went straight to Burke's office and asked the secretary outside his office if he was available. She asked who I was, I explained, and then she said, looking down at the floor to avoid the obvious awkwardness of the situation, that Mr. Marshall was not in at the moment. She referred me to his Second Assistant, St. John Barrett, who was kind enough to give me a job application. I filled it out and went home.

Three years later, in October 1966, I received a letter from an official in the Civil Rights Division notifying me that my original application had, at long last, been received. The letter had traveled from Washington to my address in Cambridge, Massachusetts, to my parents' home in New York City, and then on to me in Washington, D.C., where I was, coincidentally, already working for the Civil Rights Division. A lot had happened since I submitted that original application. I had completed my legal education, clerked for Thurgood Marshall and then for William Brennan, and, late in the summer of 1966, I had started at the Civil Rights Division. By that time John Doar, who had recruited me as a special assistant, was the Assistant Attorney General and Burke Marshall was long gone, at least physically.

Burke was then working for IBM in Armonk, New York, but John regularly conferred with him by telephone, usually in the evening. John always sat with a black notebook on his desk and took notes of the conversation. Sometimes, as with the formulation of the government's position in *Walker v. City of Birmingham*—a case arising from King's Easter 1963 campaign in Birmingham—I would sit in John's office and listen to one side of the conversation. According to John, Burke thought that the government should stress the caste-like character of the system that King was protesting. My work in the Division, and in time my mission as a professor, would be to elaborate and make more concrete Burke's insights—a task all the more difficult because I had never met the man.

After IBM, Burke joined the Yale faculty, though his route to that position was an unusual one. Late in the fall of 1964, Kingman Brewster, the relatively newly appointed President of Yale, informed—I use that

word carefully—the Law School faculty that he intended to offer Burke
Marshall the deanship of the Law School following his time at the Civil
Rights Division. The faculty received this news with a measure of un-
ease. Like Brewster, they had the highest regard for Burke and the role
he had played in shaping the civil rights policy of the federal government.
They wondered, however, whether the skills manifest in his leadership
of the Division were transferable to running an academic institution.
They were also jealous of their professorial prerogative—they believed
that it was the right of the Law School faculty, not the President of the
University, to choose the Dean. In any case, Burke Marshall was not appointed the Dean, either because the offer was never extended or because
Marshall declined it, so the conflict with the Law School faculty never
came to a head.

At that point Brewster, now acting with the concurrence of a faculty
search committee, appointed Louis Pollak to fill the vacancy, and Pollak
served as Dean from the summer of 1965 until the summer of 1970. Pollak
had been a member of the faculty for years and was active in a number
of civil rights activities. In fact, he worked with Thurgood Marshall and
the lawyers of the NAACP Legal Defense Fund on the briefs in *Brown
v. Board of Education*. In the spring of 1970, presumably at the urging of
Pollak, whose term as Dean was about to end, the Law School faculty
appointed Burke Marshall, who was then General Counsel for IBM, as a
professor of law. Burke was also appointed by Abe Goldstein, Pollak's
successor, to serve as Deputy Dean of the Law School. The Marshalls
then moved to Newtown, Connecticut.

In late 1973, a few years after Burke joined the Yale faculty and at the
height of the Watergate scandal, the Dean of the Yale Law School called
John Doar to ask whether he was prepared to work for the House Judiciary Committee and lead the inquiry into whether there were grounds
to impeach President Nixon. John said that he was. He was then appointed
to that position, and over the next seven or eight months I once again
worked for John, commuting first from Chicago and then from New
Haven. John also continued his practice of turning to Burke for advice.

John and Burke sometimes saw each other in Washington. For the most part, however, they conferred by phone.

John once again took notes on his telephone conversations with Burke in, of course, a black notebook, and my job was about the same as it had been in the Civil Rights Division: to make legal sense of Burke's reflections (although this time I felt a little more entitled to disagree with him). I always seemed to be out of town when Burke visited the offices of the Impeachment Inquiry and thus did not meet him, but John made certain to tell me of Burke's reactions to my ideas. Not all of them were favorable. I supported Article III of the Bill of Impeachment, which had made the failure of President Nixon to comply with the congressional subpoenas a ground for impeachment, but Burke thought that, too, was one of my excesses, almost an encroachment on the privilege against self-incrimination. In later years he often teased me about it.

As I was commuting between Washington and Chicago during the spring of 1974, a call came from the Dean of the Yale Law School, Abe Goldstein, inviting me to New Haven for a day of interviews for a faculty position. Job-seeking has its own set of anxieties, as everyone knows, but the ones I was experiencing then were compounded by the fact that my decade-long quest was almost over: finally, years after noticing his initials scrawled across Covington & Burling memorandums, I was going to meet Burke Marshall. In planning for my visit I asked the Dean if I might sit in on a class to get a better sense of the students, and he suggested that I attend a seminar Burke was teaching with Joe Goldstein. The seminar was entitled, in the grandiose tradition of Yale, "The Limits of Law." I asked what the seminar was about. The Dean said, also in the great Yale tradition, "I am not sure." I pressed him. Finally, he speculated, "I think it's about the legal regulation of science." At 2:10 P.M., I walked into the seminar and met Burke Marshall for the first time. He and Joe briefly introduced me to the class. It immediately became clear, however, that this was the last word they intended to say. The trap they had gleefully set was sprung—I was to conduct a class on the impeachment process then unfolding.

I had to work hard to respond to the students' questions, and to weave my responses into a coherent account of the challenges facing the Impeachment Inquiry. Almost all my attention was focused on the students. Yet I was acutely aware of the presence of Burke in the classroom; a mythical figure had become a living, breathing person. He did not say much—he never did. (His initial interview with Attorney General Robert Kennedy was legendary—apparently neither said a word to each other for the longest time, maybe for the entire interview.) During the class, Burke maintained a quiet, almost noble reserve, relieved only by an occasional shrug, a knowing smile, or a brief intervention. Yet I could almost see in his eyes the qualities of intellect and character that made him all that he was.

Burke Marshall died in June 2003 at age eighty. We were colleagues on the Yale faculty for almost thirty years, and during that time I enjoyed the marvel of Burke's friendship, mostly over lunch. He preferred hamburgers at Old Heidelberg until it became a Thai restaurant, so then we moved on to Mory's; sometimes we even indulged ourselves with a meal outdoors on the patio of Scoozzi's. Burke almost always wore a jacket and tie, and I could not help but notice that when he did his tie was fastened by the same tie clip, a replica of the patrol boat PT-109, made famous by John Kennedy.

Our luncheon conversations invariably drifted to the personal. Burke spoke about a way of life that was far removed from anything I had experienced—summers in Maine, fly fishing in the West, Christmas vacations in Tortola. He often spoke of the garden of his wife, Violet, or her latest culinary masterpiece. At one point I was struggling through the teenage years of my daughters, which seemed to go on forever. He would comfort me by talking about his own daughters and their youthful escapades. Told in retrospect, the stories were always imbued with loving amusement, as a way of assuring me that I too would survive.

Law school politics also figured in our lunches. Burke cared deeply about the school and had strong views about what should be done. Yet he was reluctant to press those views on anyone, including me. Even more remarkably, he steadfastly declined to participate in the debates that often divided the faculty. It was just not his style. He read what was to be read, and he explained his views to anyone who asked. Now and then he presented the findings of some committee he chaired, or delivered a brief report on a candidate for appointment. Yet I cannot recall any instance over our thirty years as colleagues in which he willingly, let alone eagerly, entered into the faculty fray. He sat quietly and listened. Sometimes we plotted together beforehand, and he left me with the impression that he would take the floor. I knew what he wanted to say, but in the end he would let the moment pass without a word. After each vote, which invariably allowed the Dean to have his way, Burke, with a sparkle in his eyes, chided me—why me?—because the faculty had acted, so he said, like a bunch of sheep.

Burke took teaching very seriously. He spent hours preparing for class, writing notes for himself on the assigned reading in a style that fully accorded with the Civil Rights Division tradition—in a black notebook. The case to be taught for the day or a student's response to a question was frequently the subject of our lunches. Although he had begun his career as an antitrust specialist, much to his credit he never taught the subject at Yale, for he feared the attachments that developed from his prior experience would prevent him from taking the disinterested perspective he believed teaching required.

Burke often taught procedure, and when he did, he was foolish enough to use the teaching material that Bob Cover and I, and later Judith Resnik, had been developing. When our casebook was finally published, Bill Eskridge charitably described it in the *Yale Law Journal* as "an intellectual Mardi Gras." Burke, always in control of every technical detail of a case, a lawyer par excellence, was gracious and kind, turning what must have been utter bewilderment with the material into wry amusement. Teasing me, he often asked why I had not included in our material the remarkable order issued by a federal court in the Meredith case that enjoined every sheriff in the State of Mississippi from interfering with the desegregation of Ole Miss. Since I viewed this order as an entirely appropriate exercise of the federal judicial power—certainly not Burke's view—I never had a good answer.

In the early 1980s, Burke and I embarked on a project that ultimately exceeded our collective abilities. We were joined by Renata Adler, who had recently graduated from the Law School and had written for the *New Yorker* about the South during the 1960s. The three of us believed that an important part of the truth of the civil rights era lay in the visual images that we so powerfully recalled. Photographs taken during that period memorialized the protests and marches, but they were not readily available to the new generation of lawyers (*Eyes on the Prize* did not yet exist). With the idea of publishing a collection of these photographs, framed by a text, we contacted most of the photographers who had covered the South during the early 1960s, as well as many of the leaders of the Civil Rights Movement. We also spent endless hours sifting through one archive of photographs after another. Throughout these endeavors Burke always led us to the images that revealed the nobility of those who were claiming their rights: not the turbulence, not the conflict, not the violence, though there was plenty of that, but rather the long, patient lines of Black citizens, some quite elderly, outside a polling place, waiting to vote for the first time in their lives.

This project, even more than our lunches, drew Burke back to the early 1960s, and as our relationship deepened I began to better understand the source of his greatness. Burke fully appreciated the radical nature of the change that was afoot in that period, but marveled at the thought that such dramatic change could occur both from within the law and as a response to the law. His title for the book we never published was "Revolution by Law." Burke loved the irony. Although law is often thought of as a means of maintaining order and preserving the status quo, in *Brown v. Board of Education*, he said, it performed another role altogether: law required radical change, specifically the eradication of the Jim Crow system. The law also sought to protect the protests and demonstrations that brought to fruition the very changes that the law itself had decreed.

In pointing to the remarkable, indeed unique, role law played in the civil rights era, Burke was expressing his own special understanding of law. Law for Burke was no maze of disjointed technical regulations; it had a unity and coherence because it was founded on principle. Burke was a man of the world, deeply versed in the affairs of state, and yet he never wavered in his devotion to principle. On issues of any importance, he refused to acquiesce or capitulate to practical reality. He was never, to use one of his few terms of disapproval, a "fixer." Burke fiercely and relentlessly insisted on adherence to principle. Even his conception of "a workable government," the subject of his 1987 book, was infused with that belief.

It was Burke's dedication to principle that made him so admired by those who exercised the power of the state, and even by those who took to the streets. There was an aura to his word. His judgment commanded universal respect. There were those who disagreed, especially those who fiercely resisted the changes afoot and sought to preserve the Jim Crow system, yet even they, in time, came to admire him. His devotion to principle was also manifest in his teaching. He brought his enormous real-world experience as a lawyer to the Yale Law School and then went on to demonstrate by example and word why, even in the face of the most excruciating practical pressures, there was space, and indeed a need, for principle. In this way he showed his students and his colleagues how the practice of law could be a noble profession.

Many of us were inclined to claim Burke as our hero. Burke always resisted such expressions of admiration; I would say he even cringed at them. He denied that he was anyone's hero. In so doing he may have simply been reflecting his own remarkable and very endearing modesty. Yet there was something more to his reticence. A hero, according to Burke, is someone who does more than one's duty, a person who acts in a way that no one has a right to expect or demand. Burke denied that he ever did any such thing.

For Burke, the true heroes of the civil rights era were people like James Meredith or John Hardy, or the leaders of SNCC, Bob Moses and John

Lewis, or the countless unnamed individuals, some college students, some even younger, who led voter registration drives, sat in at lunch counters, participated in the Freedom Rides, and put their lives on the line during Freedom Summer. In a review of Richard Kluger's account of the *Brown* litigation, Burke made clear his almost boundless admiration for those citizens who, in order to have standing to bring a case before a federal court, "put themselves and their families out in front of their communities and the society in which they lived." They too were heroes. Burke also spoke movingly of the lawyers—"black men and women"—who were primarily responsible for *Brown* and the cases leading up to it. As he knew all too well, these individuals were "barred at the time from jobs in the mainstream of their profession, from education in most of the nation's law schools, and, in the states where they did most of their work, from even the simplest conveniences of the life of a litigator on the road, such as a room in a good motel or a meal at a decent restaurant." (When the review that contained those words appeared in the 1976 *Harvard Law Review*, Burke received a warm congratulatory phone call from someone who, with a jovial voice, addressed him as "Cousin Marshall"—it was Thurgood Marshall.)

Those lawyers and the leaders and participants of the Civil Rights Movement were indeed heroes, according to Burke, because they took risks and made personal sacrifices that no one had any right to expect. Burke placed himself in another category altogether. True, he launched voting discrimination suits, negotiated an end to Jim Crow in many communities, used the power available to protect those who challenged the caste system, counseled the President, and shaped the Civil Rights Act of 1964 in decisive ways. These were extraordinary achievements. But Burke insisted that in all those endeavors he was only doing what was required of him as a lawyer. He did only what any lawyer should have done. He was doing his job.

On this account I might well give Burke his point and acknowledge the difference between what he did and the actions of those who led and participated in the Civil Rights Movement or who were responsible for

Brown and the early civil rights cases. If Burke was not a hero, however, it was only because he saw the profession of law in such heroic terms. He attributed his remarkable achievements to the profession to which he belonged and through which he acted. It is this vision of law—law as an emphatically principled, almost heroic endeavor—that Burke brought to the classroom and that earlier had enabled him to help guide the nation at one of the defining crossroads in its history.

II

LEGAL EDUCATION
AND THE CULTURE
OF LIBERALISM

Harry Kalven, shortly before his death in 1974 at age sixty.

5

Harry Kalven

A Tenth Justice

In the summer of 1968, upon leaving the Civil Rights Division, I joined the University of Chicago law faculty. I was hired to teach, but as soon became apparent I was also about to begin an apprenticeship with Harry Kalven, one of the leading members of the faculty and a scholar of enormous distinction.

This apprenticeship grew gradually and informally, with little self-consciousness. It began in March 1968, with a question from Harry, which was followed by a muddled answer on my part and then an intense, all-absorbing conversation—all in the Law School's freight elevator. That was during my first, bewildering day of interviews at the school. Over the years this pattern repeated itself countless times. Only the details changed. We moved out of the freight elevator and into the perennial flower garden in Jackson Park and to the lakefront at 63rd Street—places that will always have a special meaning to me because they were, in truth, Harry's classrooms.

His method was conversation. He would manage to find in the words of the apprentice glimmers of insight, which he would then restate in terms so eloquent and profound that they deepened understanding and encouraged further inquiry and comment. The apprentice felt obliged to say more, to think harder, to look at the problem from a new perspective. The conversation became an escalation of insights. That was the core of my apprenticeship with Harry. It was one of the most extraordinary experiences of my life, and it revealed the special qualities of the master.

Harry Kalven was a genius, a completely original intelligence—probably one of the few the law has ever known. My view of the world would almost always change when I listened to Harry reflect on the most recent Supreme Court decision, the latest political event, an important social institution, or the future of legal education. Perhaps one could expect that much of an eminent scholar. What I did not expect, and what was a constant source of wonder, was the fact that there were no limits to Harry's interests. He had insights into even the most trivial events.

I am not here referring to baseball. Baseball was hardly a trivial matter for Harry; it was always on his mind. He took special pride in his torts casebook because it contained so many baseball cases—indeed, he claimed, more than any other casebook. Harry grew up in Chicago and was a passionate Cubs fan. Once, he disclosed his two boyhood dreams: one was to play center field for the Chicago Cubs; the other was to speak at Rockefeller Chapel, the gorgeous, imposing cathedral on the campus of the University of Chicago. Sadly, Harry did not realize either dream, though his memorial service was held in that chapel.

I must admit that baseball was not an important part of our conversations. When he started to talk about it my eyes glazed over, and he would quickly and diplomatically change the subject. We did, however, spend hours talking about matters that most everyone else would have seen as trivial, like the practice of lining up at a gas station to refill the tank, a common occurrence in the early 1970s. Because Harry did not drive, he was usually driven around Hyde Park by his wife, Betty. One day the two of them had spent a good portion of the morning in the car waiting in line at a gas station at Lake Park and 52nd Street. Meanwhile, Stanley Katz and I were waiting at a restaurant to have lunch with him. The purpose of the lunch was to discuss the seminar on slavery and the Constitution that the three of us were to teach later that day. When Harry arrived—cheerful, totally free of annoyance—he began to reflect on the emergence of a new social institution: lining up for fuel. His focus was not on the obvious, the national energy crisis, but on the spontaneous, collective response to queue jumpers. He marveled at the cooperative nature of that response, and starting with that observation, he began to speculate about the strength of American democracy. We never did address the issues on our original agenda.

Harry had the gift not only of insight but also of expression. It was part of his genius. He turned blackboard diagramming into an art. He spoke with an ease, a grace, an eloquence that had no equal in the legal world. He wrote as he spoke, and the words he chose were the right words: not jargon, but fresh, simple words, words that lawyers had not yet exhausted or even tried. His gift of language accounts for the fact that there now exists in the law a list of phrases, including "the heckler's veto" and "the public forum," coined by Harry Kalven. These concepts were crucial in the evolution of free speech doctrine and account in part for Harry's preeminence in the field.

The phrase "uninhibited, robust, and wide-open" also makes one think immediately of Harry and his extraordinary literary sensibilities. These words were originally penned by Justice Brennan in *New York Times Co. v. Sullivan*, but it was Harry who first saw their importance in marking a new interpretation of the First Amendment, and it was Harry who, in a long series of articles starting with his classic comment on the case in the 1964 *Supreme Court Review*, immortalized them. Harry chuckled when he learned that "the Harvards"—Professors Paul Freund, Arthur Sutherland, Mark De Wolfe Howe, and Ernest Brown—edited this phrase out of Brennan's opinion when it was reprinted in their casebook.

In truth, though, Harry's intellectual stature was of minor significance to the apprentice. Genius is not a quality to which one can aspire. The apprentice can only stand in awe of it. You either have it or you don't. Harry's personal qualities, however, were another matter. They were qualities the apprentice could try to emulate and make part of his own personal code. These personal qualities drew me to Harry and became the basis of our friendship. They defined the professor that I wanted to become.

Harry Kalven once defined the law to me as "disciplined passion." He emphasized the word "passion" because it was the dimension that was too easily forgotten by the lawyer. I now realize that Harry was affirming an ideal not only for the law, but also for himself. He was a man of many passions, and they extended to the ideas that defined the liberal tradition, like liberty and equality, both because of the intellectual puzzles they posed and because he believed in their goodness.

In the 1950s, as a very young professor, Kalven became an outspoken critic of the anti-Communist crusade led by Senator Joseph McCarthy. In all his endeavors he never saw the First Amendment simply as an object of scholarly effort; to him it was an overarching ideal of personal and governmental behavior. Indeed, he often spoke of the First Amendment's "charisma." Harry also cared deeply about institutions, most notably the Supreme Court. He was repelled by the acerbic criticism of the Warren Court then commonplace in the academy, especially at Harvard but also at Chicago. Harry's analysis was as keen as anyone's, but it was distinguished by its constructive and sympathetic quality. He appreciated the heavy workload confronting the Justices and their need to find in established doctrines a path that was at once faithful to the Constitution and protective of the Court's authority in society.

Harry's sensitivity to the institutional needs of the Court informed all his commentary; and as a result, his writings, such as *The Negro and the First Amendment*, and his articles in the *Supreme Court Review*, were often regarded, on and off the bench, as the views of a tenth justice. Justice Brennan was thoroughly familiar with Kalven's work and often discussed it with me and Peter Strauss, his other clerk. Now and then the Justice even mused on the proximity of his and Kalven's views, not just on the significance of *New York Times Co. v. Sullivan*, but also on a range of free speech issues, from the regulation of pornography to the treatment of civil rights activists and their lawyers.

Another institution close to Harry's heart was the University of Chicago. It had been responsible for his entire education. He attended the elementary and high school that belonged to the University as well as its college and law school. Hour after hour we would talk about the future of the University of Chicago Law School, not because he wanted anything from it, not because it had anything more it could possibly give him, but because of his personal attachment to it and the things for which it stood. During my apprenticeship he was courted by other law schools but easily turned them down.

Harry also cared about people. His loyalty to friends was enduring and uncompromising. And he loved students. Can you imagine—a law professor of great scholarly distinction who truly loved students? His students returned the sentiment and spoke warmly of him and his classes. Occasionally they would even give him gifts, which always proved to be awkward, some more so than others.

On one occasion, after Harry had just finished the last class of the semester on free speech, and as he was walking back to his office through the student lounge, one student in the class ran up to him with a gift in hand. The student presented Harry with a large, glossy, and very vivid book that the student's father, a well-known publisher of erotica, had just released. Those who happened to be sitting in the lounge chuckled.

When Harry died at age sixty in October 1974, soon after I had left for Yale, the obituaries emphasized his age. For a man of his relative youth, his scholarly achievements were plentiful. In addition to his work on freedom of speech and torts, he made his mark on the world in a justly famous piece written with his Chicago colleague Walter Blum, "The Uneasy Case for Progressive Taxation." He was also known as one of the pioneers of integrating social science research into the law, and for years he worked with the sociologist Hans Zeisel, also a Law School colleague, on trying to measure with some precision the degree to which judges and juries could be expected to disagree on the assessment of the facts, especially in criminal cases. He found that the divergence was significantly less than was expected and concluded that the jury's distinctive contribution was to bring its sentiments about the law to bear on the fate of the accused.

When Harry died I was asked by his family to go through his papers and found in his desk a note from someone—I assumed it was Zeisel—proposing the book be called "The American Criminal Jury." Kalven, reflecting his literary sensibilities, had drawn a line through the word "Criminal," and so the book became *The American Jury*. His genius for titles was also reflected in another article he wrote with Walter Blum criticizing the pioneering work of Guido Calabresi on torts. The article's title, "The Empty Cabinet of Dr. Calabresi," was a play on a well-known silent movie from 1920, *The Cabinet of Dr. Caligari*. Harry once confessed to me that he had chosen the title two years before he wrote the article.

Harry Kalven was pleased and satisfied with what he had achieved professionally. At sixty he was a scholar of extraordinary accomplishment, yet his inclination was to look ahead, not back, and he was thrilled by the prospect of new intellectual ventures and new collaborations with a group of young upstarts. The summer before he died he had begun to formulate plans with the sociologist Stanton Wheeler to broaden and deepen his own interest in law and social science. They were to begin a study of the legal academic profession. Harry and I had discussed plans for a major new study on the pre-Civil War Constitution and the peculiar way it dealt with slavery. For him, this project was especially appealing in part because it would also involve a historian, Stanley Katz, and thus open the door to a new field of interdisciplinary study, at the intersection of law and history. In the spring of 1974, he and Gerhard Casper, a Law School colleague with a special background in political science, started another collaboration that had these same qualities, this time a study of the right to vote. To this day I distinctly recall a session of the Kalven-Casper seminar in which it dawned on Harry—with an exuberance characteristic of the discoveries of youth—that the Constitution had somehow "forgotten" the right to vote.

Kalven's youthful spirit extended to politics as well. The period of my apprenticeship with him, 1968 to 1974, was an especially turbulent era in

American history. The nation was confronted by one brutal encounter after another—the assassinations of Martin Luther King and Robert Kennedy; the rise of the Black Panthers and the efforts of the police to suppress them; the stormy protests against the Vietnam War, including demonstrations in Chicago in 1968 before the Democratic National Convention; the unruly trial in a Chicago federal court of the leaders of those demonstrations for conspiring to incite a riot; the 1970 killing by the National Guard of student antiwar protestors at Kent State University; and the 1972 break-in at the Democratic Party's national headquarters in the Watergate apartment complex, an incident which, by the summer of 1974, led to the impeachment and resignation of the President.

These events divided the nation as well as the University, and in these controversies Harry's sympathy was always with the young. He was a liberal, not a radical. He saw the complexity of issues in a way that the young often did not. Yet if forced to choose, Harry would always come down on their side. That was his impulse. He also sided with the young in the most treacherous of political affairs, university politics; it was an open secret that when, during the late 1960s and early 1970s, the "young turks" of the Law School met to plan that week's coup (never to materialize), Harry was the first to be invited.

Harry was always optimistic, determined to see, to borrow another of his favorite phrases, the "sunny side" of life and politics and also of the law. This attitude became pronounced in the seminar that Stanley Katz and I taught with Harry on the law of slavery. The broad jurisprudential question that we put to ourselves was this: How well did law stand up to the challenge posed by the existence of this thoroughly evil institution? My inclination was to be critical and severe in my judgment, perhaps too severe. Harry had a different impulse. He fought the easy answer every inch of the way, relentlessly searching for glimmers of integrity in the legal system. For the last session of our seminar, which was held in his home, Harry insisted that we all read the Thirteenth Amendment out loud.

His sunny disposition also infused Harry's work on free speech, perhaps his most enduring contribution to the liberal tradition. At the time of his death Harry left a thousand-page manuscript tracing the evolution of the Supreme Court's free speech decisions over the course of the twentieth century. He began with the disheartening decisions of the Court around World War I, when speech almost always lost. He continued through the 1930s and 1940s when, thanks to Justice Oliver Wendell Holmes's clear-and-present-danger test, speech began to win. He also chronicled the disastrous early 1950s, during the Chief Justiceship of Fred Vinson, when this test was adjusted downward in order to uphold the convictions of the leaders of the Communist Party.

Free speech took a dramatic new turn for the better, Harry felt, during the days of the Warren Court. At that time the Justices repudiated McCarthyism, curtailed the censorship of obscenity and defamation, protected civil rights activists, cut back on the possibility of prosecuting speakers for subversive advocacy, and announced in *New York Times Co. v. Sullivan* a resolve to protect robust public debate. In conversations, Harry often described the evolution of free speech doctrine during the Warren Court years as an example of "the law working itself pure."

Harry's account of the evolution of free speech doctrine struck a triumphant note when he spoke about the 1969 ruling in *Brandenburg v. Ohio*. In that case, arising from a criminal prosecution of participants in a Ku Klux Klan rally in Ohio, the Supreme Court pushed back on the reach of state censorship of subversive advocacy. In an opinion announced as a Per Curiam and endorsed by all the Justices, the Court held that even the advocacy of violence can be criminally punished only when it constitutes an "incitement to imminent lawless action" and is "likely to incite or produce such action." Soon after the Supreme Court rendered its decision in *Brandenburg v. Ohio*, Harry started to write his book on free speech. Ironically, this was also the moment when Earl Warren stepped down as Chief Justice and the other members of the liberal coalition began to retire, only to be replaced by nominees of Richard Nixon—Warren Burger, William Rehnquist, Lewis Powell, and Harry Blackmun—who were no friends of free speech.

In the summer of 1972, Harry Kalven suffered a stroke while vacationing on Martha's Vineyard (he said that God had punished him for indulging himself so luxuriously). During his convalescence over the next several months we spent hours talking about the book he had been writing. We did not dwell on the changes then taking place on the High Court or even speculate about the implications of those changes for the future of free speech. His faith in the capacity of the law to work itself pure was unshakable. The manuscript that was found on his desk when he died in 1974 bore the title *A Worthy Tradition*, fully capturing his sunny disposition.

In the final years of his life, and most certainly soon after he died, the Supreme Court's view of free speech took yet another turn. The Court denied the right of political activists to distribute leaflets in privately owned shopping centers. The Court denied state legislatures the authority to require local newspapers to provide political candidates with the right to reply to attacks on their personal character or official record. The Court denied (albeit by implication) the Federal Communications Commission the authority to require private broadcasters to cover issues of public importance and to give a balanced presentation when they did so. The Court denied the government the right to prevent corporations and the wealthy from making expenditures in elections that would drown out the voice of the poor, thereby laying the foundation for *Citizens United*.

These Supreme Court decisions can be faulted for favoring property rights over political freedom. More important, they can be faulted for denying the state any responsibility for furthering the values embodied in the First Amendment. Such a view of the state tends to reduce the liberal tradition to a set of negative commands—seeing the state only as the enemy of freedom—while ignoring the extraordinary role the state played in furthering freedom and liberal values in general during the civil rights era.

For a number of years, Jamie Kalven, Harry's son, edited the manuscript his father left unfinished. It was eventually published in 1988. I worked with Jamie on this prolonged project, and in the course of doing so often wondered what Harry would have said about the free speech doctrine then unfolding: Was this an example of the law working itself pure?

Eugene Rostow in March 1961, while Dean of the Yale Law School.

6

Eugene Rostow

The Law according to Yale

Eugene Rostow was a legendary Dean of the Yale Law School from 1955 to 1965. His first words to me came in the form of a letter he wrote in the spring of 1965 in response to an article on school desegregation I had just published in the *Harvard Law Review*. In that article I rejected the distinction between de facto and de jure segregation and argued for a constitutional duty to remedy all forms of segregation in the public schools of the nation, North and South. In the first part of his letter, Rostow embraced my argument. This was not surprising, for he had been one of the first to raise his voice against the Supreme Court's 1944 decision in the *Japanese Relocation Cases,* which he aptly called "a disaster," and his work had greatly influenced my thinking on racial discrimination. Yet the second part of his letter was critical, and initially puzzling.

Gene's criticism stemmed from what he believed was a shortcoming in my education. I had started the article in the fall of 1963 as a student at the Harvard Law School. Although the nation was being swept by the Civil Rights Movement and the struggle for racial equality, Harvard's intellectual milieu was defined by Herbert Wechsler's 1959 article on neutral principles, in which he announced that he had come to the conclusion that *Brown v. Board of Education* was wrongly decided, or at least not adequately justified. Wechsler, a scholar of enormous prestige, taught at Columbia Law School, but his spirit filled the classrooms of Harvard. His article on neutral principles appeared in the *Harvard Law Review;* it was first delivered as part of the prestigious Holmes lecture series at Harvard. Aside from that article, Wechsler was largely known to us from his casebook *Federal Courts,* which he wrote with Henry Hart, one of Harvard's most revered intellectual figures during my time there.

Yale had a very different stance on *Brown*—it embraced the decision. In 1952, shortly before becoming Dean, Gene himself had forcefully written in defense of judicial review, and in that context praised the civil rights decisions of the Supreme Court that eventually paved the way to the *Brown* decision in 1954. The defense of *Brown* specifically, was taken up by two of his faculty, Charles Black and Louis Pollak, both of whom had worked with Thurgood Marshall on the briefs in that case. One could not help but be moved by the eloquence and logic of Black's and Pollak's accounts of *Brown.* To this day, I can remember the thrill of reading their articles for the first time.

Even after reading Black's and Pollak's articles, though, I found it necessary, as I worked on my paper in the stacks of Langdell Hall in 1963, to return to Wechsler's argument and to demonstrate that *Brown* was consistent with, indeed compelled by, a proper application of the neutral principles that Wechsler had extolled. The point of my article was, after all, to move *Brown* from the South to the nation at large, and in order to do that I thought it necessary to prove once again that *Brown* was rightly decided.

Rostow thought such an exercise was unnecessary. In the second, critical part of his letter, he chided me for taking Wechsler's account of neutral principles too seriously. He was not asking me to accept on faith what scholars like Black and Pollak had said—as I later came to learn, Gene loved nothing more than a good argument—but he was expressing his pride of place. He resented that I had let Harvard dictate the terms of my inquiry. Although he made allowances for my educational "handicap" (his familiar twinkle was evident between the lines), these allowances paled against the intense pride that Rostow felt for Yale and the liberal tradition with which it had become identified. Gene's letter was written just as he was finishing his ten-year term as Dean of the Yale Law School, during which the Law School emerged as a great national institution, a bastion of the liberal tradition. In his criticism of my article Rostow was, in effect, affirming his belief in both the preeminence of Yale and the triumph of liberalism while expressing his regret that I had not seen it that way—not yet anyway.

Eugene Rostow had a long involvement with the Yale Law School. Before becoming Dean he was a student at the school and then a professor. After stepping down from the deanship, he served in the State Department from 1966 to 1969 as Under Secretary for Political Affairs, thoroughly involved with the stormy challenges presented by the Vietnam War. At the end of those years at the State Department, he briefly returned to Yale to teach, but by the late 1970s, Rostow had moved back to Washington and continued his involvement in the foreign and diplomatic affairs of the nation. He founded the Committee on the Present Danger, a foreign policy advocacy group, and later briefly served in the Reagan administration in charge of nuclear disarmament. He formally retired from the Law School in 1984 and died at age eighty-nine in 2002.

I came to Yale in the mid-1970s, after teaching at the University of Chicago for six years. As I might have expected from his initial letter, Gene warmly welcomed me to the Law School, though in one instance this warmth took an unusual turn. He and his wife, Edna, invited me and my wife to have dinner with the members of his Yale Law School class, who were in town for the annual alumni weekend. The dinner at the Quinnipiack Club was relaxing and jovial—until we were finishing dessert, at which time Gene stood up and announced, to my utter surprise, that a young new member of the faculty would now address them. God only knows what I said for the next thirty minutes. When I sat down, somewhat flustered, Edna chided Gene for putting me on the spot. Gene only smiled and said that every young man should be put to such a test—which, of course, is true.

My tenure and Gene's at Yale overlapped for only about five years. Even before he returned to Washington, Gene had begun to turn away from the internal affairs of the Law School. His experience at the State Department during the Vietnam years had sharpened his interest in foreign affairs, and by the time I joined the Yale faculty in 1974 he saw himself as an actor on the world stage. As a result, I largely had to discover for myself the dynamics that made the Law School what it had become. I undertook this task over the next forty years with the unique passion of a convert, sometimes losing sight of where Gene's ideas about the school ended and mine began.

Any account of the fortunes of the Yale Law School must begin by recognizing that there is an excitement to legal education in the United States that is often lacking in the nation's great graduate departments. Admittedly, some of this excitement stems from extrinsic factors: the prestigious and relatively high-paying jobs available to law students; the intensive, interactive pedagogic technique (although the so-called Socratic method, at least in its brutal *Paper Chase* form, is rarely practiced at Yale); and the eclectic, indelible personalities of the faculty (no doubt found in abundance at the Law School). I suspect, however, that the key to success in legal education—not just at Yale but at all American law schools—is intrinsic to the subject matter. Law is an unusual blend of the academic and the professional. Legal education requires that the insights of the many disciplines taught in graduate school—sociology, history, philosophy, psychology, politics, economics, for example—be brought to bear in a focused way on discrete, concrete problems confronted by professionals in the exercise of power.

Yale's distinguishing feature stems from its emphasis, propounded throughout Gene's deanship, on bringing a scholarly perspective to the law. In describing Yale this way, and perhaps even daring to call it an academic law school, I am not referring to the career patterns of its graduates. Granted, an enormously disproportionate number of America's law teachers come from Yale, and the school accepts a special responsibility in preparing students for academia. Would-be teachers, however, constitute a relatively small share of each class. The vast bulk of Yale's graduates become practicing lawyers. The academic character of the school is rooted in the fact that it offers students, all students, an education designed to foster a broad, critical perspective on the law—a perspective most often associated with a scholar.

The Law School's governing assumption is that its students will spend their lives fully engaged in exercising the power of the law. But of course lawyering takes many forms. Advocacy on behalf of a narrow set of interests—advocacy in the style of Perry Mason—is only one among many forms of engagement. Some of Yale's graduates will be judges; some will be legislators; some will be government lawyers, prosecuting cases on behalf of the United States; some will represent the great private enterprises of the day; some will be engaged in international trade; some will work toward world peace; some will lead administrative agencies; some will become "public interest" lawyers.

In all of these endeavors, lawyers must master the technical details of the law so that they can manipulate the levers that govern the exercise of power. Yet lawyers must also be able to reflect on the ends of the legal system and to design institutions that fulfill those ends. Is it any wonder then that the Yale curriculum—to take a sample from one year's course catalogue—includes classes called "Tragic Choices," "The Political Philosophy of Hannah Arendt," "The Limits of Law as an Instrument of Social Control," "Nuclear Arms Control," "Theories of Contract," "Immigration and National Purpose," "Public Order of the World Community," "Alternatives in Enterprise Organization," "Psychoanalytic and Legal Perspectives on Attorney-Client Relations," "Toxic Chemicals," and "Myth, Law, and History?"

The school is not unmindful of the role that lawyers play as advocates, yet even from that perspective an academic approach seems essential to a proper legal education. Advocacy is more than the mere manipulation of rules to serve a client's interest. For one thing, advocates often must define and identify just what a client's interests are, especially when the client happens to be a political group, corporation, union, government agency, or some other large, complex organization. In such cases, lawyers must decide who speaks for the organization and how internal conflicts that divide the client are to be resolved.

Effective advocacy also demands an understanding of the broader purpose behind each rule and doctrine. A lawyer cannot, for instance, effectively represent a client in an antitrust case without understanding economic theory or the history of the Sherman Act. Even more, the advocacy that society allows a lawyer is a limited one, and the effective advocate must understand those limits. Some limits can be found in criminal statutes, liability rules, and professional canons. But the most important ones are derived from the dictates of justice or from a broad understanding of the lawyer's role in society. These general, open-ended commitments vary from time to time, and from context to context, and they cannot be understood without regard for the teachings of moral philosophy, economics, sociology, political science, history, and perhaps even theology.

None of this obviates the need for training in more traditional legal skills. To take the most obvious example (and the one closest to my heart), Yale has always had a required first-year course on procedure. Students are expected to master the technical rules of procedure, and for that purpose they are given an opportunity to draft pleadings, work through discovery problems, write briefs, and argue cases. It would be a sad irony, indeed, if Yale's scholarly emphasis, which began as a way of broadening the lawyer's perspective, became its own peculiar source of narrowness. Training in the technical skills of advocacy might be necessary, but it is not sufficient.

Skills training must be only a part of a larger, much more intellectually ambitious procedure course, one that compares the rules of various procedural systems and examines the relation between the substantive ends of the law and its procedural rules. On a more heretical note (given that Charles Clark, author of the Federal Rules of Civil Procedure, was once the Dean of Yale), such a course must ask whether the arrangements that produced today's federal procedural rules are either wise or constitutional. The structure of law is indeed embedded in the intricate details of written rules and regulations, and a mastery of those details is essential for any general inquiry. Yet an academic law school, the sort of school Gene Rostow helped build, insists (maybe "hopes" is the better word) that more theoretical inquiries be at the center of the educational enterprise, and that the mastery of the specific be in the service of the general.

Ultimately, the quality of any educational institution depends on the depth and range of its faculty. The faculty shapes the curriculum and is responsible for the institution's scholarly output, the character of its library, the kinds of students it attracts. It is the faculty who define the school. Eugene Rostow knew this, and he tried to teach it to me. In 1975, Harry Wellington was appointed Dean of the Law School, and in the early years of his administration I was asked to consider ways the procedures that governed the school might be changed. In response, I came up with a scheme to have a faculty member other than the Dean lead the process for selecting and hiring teachers. When I proposed this idea to Gene in a discussion over lunch at Mory's, he convinced me, in no uncertain terms, of the foolishness of this idea.

Making faculty appointments is a time-consuming endeavor, for it requires keeping up with the work of promising new scholars; yet in Gene's view building and rebuilding the faculty constituted the Dean's highest duty. Indeed, this was the guiding precept of his own administration. During his deanship Gene increased the size of the faculty by one third, and in the late 1950s brought to the Law School a remarkable group of young scholars, affectionately known as "Rostow's Dozen," who built on the traditions of the school and, over the next several decades, created several of Yale's many golden ages.

Although faculty appointments are indeed crucial, an institution's character is not reducible to the people who populate it. The institution also shapes the character of the people in it. The Yale faculty consists of strong-minded and independent scholars, but no one can deny the influence of the Law School as an institution on its faculty's research agenda, their course offerings, their methods of inquiry, and even their worldviews. This influence is felt in many ways. One is through the transmission of its ideals. Yale's pursuit of an academic perspective guides staffing policy; it shapes who is invited to join the faculty and who accepts that invitation. It explains why Yale's faculty have included so many who have had graduate or professional training in economics, philosophy, political science, history, psychology, and sociology—though none of us perceives the absence of such training as a limitation on our capacity to profess on those subjects.

The academic aspirations of Yale are also reflected in the size of the faculty: the Law School has one of the most favorable student-faculty ratios in the nation. To some, Yale's ratio may seem to be a function of its riches, but in truth, as can be seen from a comparison with a law school of equal resources (Harvard), the insistence on a highly favorable faculty-student ratio stems from the understanding that the kind of writing and research that is at the heart of an academic endeavor can only take place in small settings. To this end, Yale places every first-year student in a class of seventeen, an appropriate setting for an intensive introduction to legal writing. This practice continues in the advanced curriculum, which is distinguished by a proliferation of seminars, some with only a handful of students.

The ideals of the institution also define, in subtle and complex ways, the scholarly and pedagogic ambitions of the faculty. No one could be at Yale for long without recognizing that the faculty are expected to produce something more than practitioners' digests. They are expected to craft meditations on the purposes of the law and to produce magical syntheses—always slightly beyond our reach—of the technical and theoretical aspects of legal doctrine. In my years at Chicago, I wrote extensively about civil rights litigation, but when I joined the Yale faculty I started, for better or worse, writing articles with titles like "The Jurisprudence of Busing," and "Groups and the Equal Protection Clause," and from there moved on to "The Forms of Justice."

The influence of the institution is also felt through dynamics and practices that make Yale feel something like an organized anarchy. To be sure, most law schools honor academic freedom in matters of scholarship.

At Yale, though, this ethos is extended to the classroom, allowing each professor the freedom—relinquished only at the rarest moments—to decide what to teach, how to teach, even when to teach. The faculty believe that teaching makes the same demands on one's creative capacities as scholarship. They also believe that there is an essential unity of teaching and scholarship. The classroom is a workshop from which scholarship springs, and to which it returns.

There are, of course, drawbacks to this freedom. There are virtually no classes offered on Friday afternoons. There is also an appearance of redundancy. One semester there were five seminars offered on judicial review (several called just that, and others hidden behind Yale-sounding euphemisms such as "Constitutional Theory" or "Slavery, the Constitution, and the Supreme Court"). But the problem of overlap is of no special concern to the faculty because it seems to be an issue of form rather than substance. At Yale the essential educational experience consists of the exchange of ideas between students and faculty, and the character and quality of that exchange depend on what each participant has to say. Every member of the faculty could teach a course on judicial review, and indeed use the same cases and material, and yet, I can assure you, there would be no true redundancy.

In contrast to the problem of overlap, the issue of gaps is a substantial one. For many years, for instance, Yale did not offer even a basic course on patents or on financial institutions; today, there is none on admiralty. The problem of gaps is especially worrisome if the concern is not just with areas of law but with analytic techniques (such as statistics), or if we look to the future and consider the needs of lawyers who will reach the peak of their careers well into the future, twenty-five years after graduation. Subjects that in all rights should be taught may simply never appear in the Yale catalogue, and the question then becomes what should be done in response.

Unfortunately, there are no simple solutions, especially in an institution that takes pride in the creative achievements of its faculty. It would make no sense to abandon the instructional freedom that belongs to every professor and to allow the Dean, or even worse, some committee, to assign the faculty to particular courses. Such an arrangement would require, at a minimum, collective agreement on the gaps that must be filled. Yet given the very strong and disparate views on exactly what is missing, that would be an almost impossible task. Even if the gaps were adequately identified, filling them could require the school to rely on reluctant (and perhaps unqualified) recruits, thereby ignoring the subtle, somewhat fragile dynamic between student, teacher, and subject matter that is the core of effective teaching. Students learn from the love a teacher brings to his or her subject and from the kind of curiosity that such love engenders.

The solution to the problem of gaps, therefore, lies not in the surrender of one's freedom to some central authority, but in a recognition by each professor of a responsibility for the education of the students. This sense of responsibility must be reflected in the courses offered and in the range of scholarly interests represented on the faculty, knowing full well that the faculty will never be large enough to teach all that must be learned. The Dean must lead, not by issuing ukases, which at best would be counterproductive, but by cultivating and strengthening in the faculty a sense of responsibility for the curriculum. Anarchists also emphasize individual responsibility in an effort to assure their followers that a turn away from the state will not result in chaos. Although such reassurances seem hollow in the context of the modern nation-state, this is not true with law schools, which are infinitely more intimate communities, and where the stakeholders are bound together by a common mission.

A final consequence of the pedagogic freedom that Yale celebrates is that it is especially difficult for a student to construct a sequence of courses that leads to a progressively greater proficiency in a particular subject. During Rostow's deanship the desire to let students cumulate knowledge and develop a measure of expertise led to the Divisional Program, which sought to organize the faculty into mini-departments responsible for various fields of study. Even this minimal structure, however, proved too intrusive. By the late 1970s all that remained of the Divisional Program was the requirement that every student write two extended papers before graduation, including one that involves substantial student research under faculty supervision. At its best, the emphasis on writing allows the student to acquire the depth promised by an institutionally imposed sequence of courses while, at the same time, acknowledging the individualism that inheres in the creative processes that lie at the core of both teaching and learning.

Yale is not, of course, all anarchy. Some institutional structures do emphasize the communal nature of the school's educational enterprise. I am referring not to the obligation to report course offerings to the Registrar, nor the occasional committee meeting—they are in truth trivial—but to those occasions that gather the faculty for discussions—morning coffee, lunch, and perhaps most importantly, faculty workshops where articles and books in progress are considered.

During Rostow's deanship, the principal faculty workshop was called the Non-Hohfeld Society, a play on the name of Wesley Newcomb Hohfeld, a philosopher on the Yale faculty in the early twentieth century known for his elaborate but somewhat tedious taxonomy of basic legal concepts such as "duty" and "liberty." This workshop was only occasionally convened, usually to vet some prospect for a faculty position. Imbued with more grandiose ambitions, Bruce Ackerman and I established the Legal Theory Workshop in 1974, when we first joined the Yale faculty. As originally conceived, this workshop met bi-weekly throughout the academic year, and in order to keep the focus on ideas, it was never allowed to become an adjunct to the appointments process. Although we by and large only invited scholars from other universities to present their work in progress, we deliberately avoided inviting anyone who was being considered or likely to be considered for a Yale appointment. The Legal Theory Workshop has been replicated at other law schools and through the leadership of other members of the faculty, continues at the Law School to this day. Over the years, the Yale faculty developed workshops on law and economics, legal history, and human rights, as well as one devoted exclusively to the presentation of the faculty's own work in progress.

Serious intellectual discussion among colleagues is difficult to sustain. Everyone is very busy, and the individualism celebrated in academic endeavors necessarily draws people in different directions. Sometimes the only common denominator is the daily newspaper. So, while the ostensible function of the school's workshops is to provide scholars (from Yale and other universities) with a forum in which to present and refine their work in progress, its true value is in sparking discussion among the Yale faculty, not just when the workshop meets formally, but also in the days before and after. The work presented in the workshops provide the common text necessary to stimulate serious and reasoned discussion among colleagues. It is a welcome substitute for the *New York Times* or the latest movie.

Discussing ideas, I am duty-bound to admit, is fun. It relieves some of the loneliness inherent in academic life. It is also a form of continuing education, a source of intellectual renewal and growth. We are forced to reexamine our premises, learn about new developments in other fields (and sometimes even in our own), and combat the narrowness and staleness that can infect academic inquiry. For most of us, our formal education and professional training ended some twenty or thirty years ago. We are in constant danger of becoming obsolete, and as though that were not enough, we are often tempted to narrow our focus in order to maintain our mastery of increasingly complex subjects. It therefore seems imperative, if we are to do justice to our fields and to ourselves, to find ways to broaden our horizons and renew our critical capacities.

Reading helps. So does the constant influx of young people into our classrooms. Some of us even take courses elsewhere in the University. It seems to me, however, that a vital engine of renewal and growth consists of the discussion that goes on at faculty workshops, at lunch, and in the corridors of the Law School. As a form of continuing education for educators, these discussions are compelling: they honor the collegial character of the faculty and convey their lessons with an immediacy and vibrancy that can stir even those who purport to speak with authority. Serious discussions among colleagues emphasize the democratic character of the educational process. They are true to Rostow's vision of legal education and even of his understanding of the essential dynamics of the political community.

In his 1952 article on the Supreme Court entitled "The Democratic Character of Judicial Review," Rostow defended a conception of the judiciary that was soon to be manifested in the work of the Warren Court. He believed that "American life in all its aspects is an attempt to express and to fulfill a far-reaching moral code," and further that the wise but strong exercise of power by the judiciary would release and encourage "the dominantly democratic forces of American life." In making this claim, Rostow was aware of the 1937 Court-packing debacle provoked by the Supreme Court's initial response to the New Deal; but he put the regulatory disputes responsible for that confrontation between the political branches and the judiciary to one side and insisted that cases involving civil rights, criminal procedure, and free speech were of an entirely different order.

Rostow wrote the article at a time when the country was in the grips of McCarthyism and the political freedom of Americans was at risk. He had harsh words for the Supreme Court's 1951 decision in *Dennis v. United States*, which upheld the conviction under the Smith Act of the leaders of the Communist Party. He praised the dissent in that case of Justice William Douglas (once a member of the Yale faculty) and faulted the decision of the majority for confusing a political party with a conspiracy to overthrow the government. Rostow's criticism was not confined to the Justices who signed on to *Dennis*; it also extended to Judge Learned Hand, who had written the opinion for the Second Circuit in the case and who had manipulated, or at least adjusted, the clear-and-present-danger test in such a way as to facilitate the affirmance of the convictions. Hand reasoned that the severity of the danger allowed the judiciary to all but disregard the inquiry into whether the danger was clear or present.

Dennis was not Hand's only sin. He also propounded a general theory about judicial review that guided or at least accorded with his action in that case, essentially emasculating the judiciary when called upon to give force to the principles of liberty and equality in the Bill of Rights and the Civil War amendments. Hand set forth his theory in a 1942 speech in Boston celebrating the 250th anniversary of the Supreme Judicial Court of Massachusetts—the oldest court in continuous existence in America. His talk, "The Contribution of an Independent Judiciary to Civilization," was reprinted in 1952 in a book edited by Irving Dilliard, *The Spirit of Liberty*. For more than half a century his words have been celebrated and used by conservatives of all stripes.

Hand's theory was premised on a distinction between two types of constitutional provisions: those that "distribute the powers of government" and those that "lay down general principles to ensure the just exercises of those powers." With respect to the second category of constitutional provisions, Hand insisted, with a rhetorical flourish unequaled in the law, that the judiciary could do little to restrain society or its political agents from acting on their understandings of the "fundamental principles of equity and fair play," that the powers of the judiciary would be curbed if it sought to interfere with such actions, and that in any event, any effort by the judiciary to prevent the political institutions from acting on their own understandings of such principles would undermine or erode the sense of responsibility that these institutions might have for the moral progress of society.

In no uncertain terms Rostow dismissed Hand's views as "gloomy and apocalyptic," reflecting "the dark shadows thrown upon the judiciary by the Court-packing fight of 1937." Rostow saw—even without the benefit of *Brown* and the revolution that it inspired—how the Supreme Court might play a positive role in the formation of public opinion and in the elaboration of the "moral code" that lies at the heart of American civilization. He also spoke of the salutary influence that the Court has had over the years on many social and political institutions, not just Congress and the President, but also the press, political parties, scholars, and interest groups. In a sentence long remembered by the generation of legal scholars who, like me, began their careers in the wake of *Brown*, Rostow declared, "The Supreme Court is, among other things, an educational body, and the Justices are inevitably teachers in a vital national seminar." In responding to Hand in this way, Rostow was projecting onto the body politic, and onto the debates about the legitimacy of judicial review, an understanding of academic life—the give and take of "a vital national seminar"—that he sought to create and nurture at Yale and that perhaps constitutes its most distinguishing feature.

Arthur Leff in the spring of 1979, on the occasion of being named the Southmayd Professor of Law.

7

Arthur
Leff

Making Coffee and Other Duties of Citizenship

He died young. Arthur Leff died in 1981 at the age of forty-six. He had joined the Yale law faculty in 1968 and for the next thirteen years was sustained and nurtured by the school. Art's talents and abilities were truly original, almost idiosyncratic, and it is a measure of Yale's greatness that it was able to evoke in such a dedicated and busy scholar not just service and loyalty, but also a deep affection. Arthur Leff returned Yale's high regard for him with a light-hearted, cheerful, and loving devotion, and in time he became an extraordinary citizen of the school.

Citizenship in an academic institution is a high and difficult art. The Yale Law School is no different. The difficulty stems largely from the peculiar character of such an institution: it is an entity that transcends any individual, yet at its core it is defined by individual creative capacities. We speak of communal goals—the education of professionals or the shared pursuit of truth—but we know the attainment of those goals depends on profoundly individualistic activities. Scholarship is lonely; so is teaching. Each depends on the expression of talents and capacities that are individually possessed; each requires a self-conceived, self-imposed discipline; each involves engagement in activities, like reading books, that must be done alone; each requires individuals to worry ideas to the point of exhaustion and then to forge them into coherent, persuasive, and distinctive positions.

There is a collective dimension to the Law School, to be sure, but this does not deny the centrality of the individual. Rather, the collective dimension of the school is a resource for individual creativity. It helps us turn our loneliness to productive ends. It provides us with classrooms and students and books, and with economic resources that will free our time. It embodies and transmits the ideals of the profession; it presents us with talented and dedicated colleagues. In this way the school is a communal enterprise dedicated to individual fulfillment—as I said in Chapter 6, it is an organized anarchy—and the citizenship it invites reflects the institution's complicated, somewhat contradictory nature.

At times, though only rarely, the Law School imposes some uniform obligations: a standard teaching load (never defined with precision at Yale) and the usual array of committee assignments. These obligations are not very demanding—no standard obligation can be. They are the minimum, and the sad truth is that for many of us the minimum becomes the maximum. Not so for Art. He impeccably discharged the minimum obligations and then went far beyond them. He realized that these standard exactions were trivial and that if Yale was to achieve its grandest purposes more would be required—much more. He realized, for example, that someone had to make the coffee.

When I came to the Yale Law School from the University of Chicago in 1974, Art was only in his late thirties, yet he had already achieved a measure of distinction. He was known, even at Chicago, as one of Yale's most popular teachers. He had already made important contributions to contract law. In 1967 and again in 1970, he published two major articles on contracts—"Unconscionability and the Code: The Emperor's New Clause," and "Contract as Thing." These works displayed a doctrinal virtuosity, yet at the same time were sensitive to the challenges introduced by modern commercial transactions. In the end they argued for more robust public oversight to protect consumers.

In the spring of 1974, Art published a review of Richard Posner's *Economic Analysis of Law*, a book that had already created quite a stir and would soon become a foundation for the Law and Economics movement. In this book Posner insisted that over a large range of categories—from property to racial discrimination to civil procedure to criminal law—legal doctrine should be understood as promoting "efficiency," which he narrowly defined as the allocation of "economic resources in such a way that human satisfaction as measured by aggregate consumer willingness to pay for goods and services is maximized."

Leff sharply criticized this vision. He began by wryly observing that Posner's book seemed closest in genre to *Huckleberry Finn*, a "picaresque novel" in which the "hero sets out into a world of complexity and brings to bear on successive segments of it the power of his own particular personal vision." More substantively, Leff argued that the book was "four hundred pages of tunnel vision" and that Posner's analysis was itself based on "assumptions" as arbitrary as any in legal academia.

On the basis of these works, the image I had of Art from afar was exalted indeed. I therefore was quite surprised when, in the fall of 1974, during my first days at Yale, I found him in the faculty lounge deeply absorbed in the process of making coffee. He was focused, moving with dispatch and seemingly with pleasure. I was, to say the least, puzzled. He reassured me that I had not come to the wrong place and proudly explained that his campaign to obtain the coffeemaker for the faculty lounge had been his most important contribution to the world of ideas.

The coffee was, of course, simply a prop. Art's talk about making coffee was a modest way of expressing the central tenet of his theory of citizenship: the highest duty of the citizen-scholar was to talk about ideas with others. So Art made himself available. He was available in the faculty lounge for conversation in the morning. He was available for lunch (with one or two forgivable lapses for squash). He was again available in the lounge in the late afternoon to continue the discussion begun earlier that day or weeks before. He was a regular at the organized evening conversations of the faculty sponsored by the Legal Theory Workshop. In fact, Art helped establish the one law that governed the workshop, the law of inverse relationship, which holds that the weaker the paper the better the discussion will be among those in the audience.

The need for someone to make coffee was especially pronounced during the 1970s. In October 1974, after a long illness, Alexander Bickel died, at age forty-nine, of brain cancer. He was the most prominent constitutional lawyer of his generation and played a dominant, all-pervasive role in the internal politics of the Law School during the turbulent late 1960s and early 1970s. The loss of Bickel was felt by the nation at large, but it reverberated in the corridors of the Law School with particular pathos. Bickel's death was a tragic reminder of the losses the Yale faculty suffered soon after Leff's appointment in 1968. It also foreshadowed the losses that were to follow in the next year or two.

During this period a number of senior faculty retired—Myres McDougal, Thomas Emerson, and James William Moore. Louis Pollak transferred to the University of Pennsylvania, and Clyde Summers soon joined him. Ronald Dworkin left for Oxford. Robert Bork took an extended leave from the Law School to serve as Solicitor General in the Nixon and Ford administrations. Charles Reich quit teaching law altogether and moved to the San Francisco area.

At roughly the same time, many of the younger faculty were denied tenure and relocated. John Griffiths moved to Holland, George Lefcoe returned to the University of Southern California, and Larry Simon joined him there. Rick Abel went to UCLA, Bob Hudec joined the University of Minnesota faculty, Lee Albert took a position at SUNY Buffalo, and David Trubek went to the University of Wisconsin. John Ely was promoted, but in 1973 he left Yale and joined the Harvard faculty.

In the face of those losses the Yale faculty started the process of rebuilding and for that purpose appointed several younger law teachers: Robert Cover, Alvin Klevorick, John Baker, Bruce Ackerman, Barbara

Underwood, Robert Burt, Jerry Mashaw, Paul Gewirtz, and me. Art Leff, who had been recruited to Yale in 1968 in his mid-thirties, was a vital force in this younger group of teachers. He was widely respected by his elders—as far as I know, he was the only one of the younger generation who was invited to join the elders' long-running weekly poker game. Yet it was among the newly recruited younger generation that he played his most decisive role. He was at the center of this group, admired and liked by all of us. We all counted on him to make the coffee.

There was a strong tradition among our generation to circulate drafts of papers for comments. The draft was always received with the promise "I'll get back to you," but sometimes work piled up and the promise remained undelivered. Not so for Art. He always found time to read the drafts. He also had a knack for criticizing a draft in a way that was true to his intellectual standards and that nonetheless made the author feel good about herself or himself (talk about a high and difficult art). Art was careful, patient, and very generous. He was the only person in the group who read all thirty-two revisions of Bruce Ackerman's manuscript for *Social Justice in the Liberal State*, and he got a kick out of each one.

In these activities Art grasped an essential truth about the Law School, and about scholarship and teaching in general. Scholarship and teaching are indeed lonely, but until words appear in print or a sentence is uttered in class, there is a place and a need for the kind of support, encouragement, and help that only a community of intellectuals can provide for one another. Yale was, for Art, such a community, and he was determined to mobilize its every capacity. He did so by making coffee—by talking about ideas in a way that made participation by others irresistible.

I must also acknowledge that Art sought pleasure. He talked about ideas because he thought it was fun. He delighted in ideas. He loved to learn something new or to hear an old argument reformulated. There was, as he said, a special joy in having something true truly put. I believe, however, that there was more to Art's civic activity and his talk about ideas than a desire to have fun or to satisfy his own curiosity. He also acted from a sense of duty that emphasized the responsibility of the members of an academic community to engage in serious talk about ideas.

Art was motivated in his civic activities by a broad-ranging curiosity. There was no subject, no field of learning, scientific or humanistic, that was not of interest to him. Dick Posner once complained to me of the impossible standards Art had imposed in the review of *Economic Analysis of Law* that I mentioned. It was not enough, Dick quipped, for the legal scholar to become an economist; he also had to become an anthropologist, a sociologist, and even a psychologist (in time, Dick became all those things, but not, I fear, in the way Art had contemplated).

Art died of lung cancer. In his final weeks, as he sat in his living room, many of us visited him there. It was hard for him to speak, and now and then, when he needed a rest, he would pause and glance out the window. The visitor might continue talking, but soon he too would stop and glance around the room. What the visitor would then see was truly a monument to liberal education: shelves and shelves of books—beautiful books, alluring books, well-thumbed books—from almost every field of learning. Arthur Leff was the most liberally educated person I knew.

Art was a sensationally successful teacher. The students loved him, and they had good reason to. He was witty, lively, even entertaining. He was also demanding. He proved that it was possible to be both funny and learned. He achieved acclaim in all the pedagogic formats that have yet been devised by the Yale mind: the large section, the small group, the lecture course, the seminar, and the reading group, that occult curricular entity that spontaneously formed around Arthur Leff each year and that met from week to week at such elegant lecture halls as Yorkside Pizza. I was curious about his extraordinary success and, I should probably admit, somewhat envious. I pressed Art for his secrets.

One day I asked what led him to include a course on evidence in his repertoire. I knew of no one who taught both contracts and evidence and wondered whether teaching a more diverse selection of courses might be the key to the success for which I was searching. His explanation was quite simple. He had asked the Dean to prepare a list of courses that should be covered if we were to fulfill our responsibility as a law school. The Dean obliged (eagerly, I am sure, since the list was long), and Art chose the evidence course from the Dean's list. I responded to this explanation with utter amazement. Had Yale's finest citizen committed treason? Imagine discussing a teaching program with the Dean? The Registrar maybe, but never the Dean. I was reeling in disbelief. My temperature rose and my face became flushed. Art tried, as he did on so many occasions, to calm me. He quickly assured me that he was not recommending this process for anyone else. Besides, he said, he enjoyed teaching the course.

Art could sometimes seem indifferent to the grand issues of the day. During the late 1970s the legal academy was deeply divided. Some complained of the newly constituted Supreme Court's program to eradicate the legacy of the Warren Court. While the followers of Law and Economics grew in number, echoing Posner's proclamation that "law is efficiency," a new, leftist movement—Critical Legal Studies— emerged, proclaiming "law is politics." At roughly the same time, feminism established a beachhead in the legal academy. Catharine MacKinnon published *Sexual Harassment of Working Women*, condemning a familiar social practice that treated women as sex objects. Amidst these turbulent cross currents, Arthur Leff decided to write a dictionary. To be sure, the dictionary would be an unusual one, more learned and opinionated than any other—but still, a dictionary. Although he never completed the dictionary, excerpts from the manuscript were published posthumously in the *Yale Law Journal*. The image of indifference that Art projected by his decision to write a dictionary sometimes veered off in the direction of nihilism, though I believe he was often just trying to get a rise out of his colleagues.

When Art gave me a reprint of his justly celebrated 1979 article "Unspeakable Ethics, Unnatural Law," he said that the entire range of ethical views represented in Western civilization could be mapped on the second-floor corridor of the Law School. At one end was me and my search for absolutes; in the middle was Bruce Ackerman and his engagement in what might be called "liberal dialogue." At the head of the corridor was Art's office, which he tried to convince me was some sort of nihilist's abyss. That corridor, incidentally, also came close to being a map of the Bronx. Art, Bruce, and I each grew up in the Bronx during the same era, but the difference between us was as vast as the differences between the neighborhoods of our childhood: Pelham Bay (me), Girard Avenue (Bruce), and the Grand Concourse (Art).

My reaction to Art's jurisprudence was predictable. I often told him that he was only pulling my leg—his professed nihilism was so inconsistent with all that I knew about him. You can imagine what he said about my search for objective truth. I will leave it to others to determine who was fooling whom, but I insist that when it came to the important matters—to Art's relationship with other people, to the political issues that divided the nation, or to the quality of academic life—there was not a trace of indifference. About those matters Arthur Leff cared deeply.

Indeed, the personal qualities of Art that some may have viewed as indifference were in truth of a wholly different character. He treated everyone—faculty, students, and staff—with the greatest respect. Art appreciated each individual's needs and concerns and was exceedingly tolerant of differences and idiosyncrasies. I never heard him say a mean word about anyone. Never. He accepted people as they were and was determined to see the best in everyone, and even more, to bring out their best. Art also was very funny. While many of us would express our disappointment with a sharp word or a long face, Art typically coped with such situations with a shrug of his shoulders, an angelic smile, or a sparkling one-liner.

Tolerance and respect are required for an academic community; humor is not, and neither is music. Art loved music, and a few years before he died he placed a stereo system in his office. He had always kept his door open as a way of signaling to his colleagues that he was available for conversation, and he continued that practice even after installing the stereo. Careful not to impose his musical tastes on others, he simply donned a set of earphones. So, day in and day out, Arthur Leff sat hunched over his desk, compiling his law dictionary while listening to music through his earphones—conveying a Dali-like image of the contemporary dictionary writer caught in a web of words and wires. Most of the time he kept the beat with a pencil—*res ipsa loquitur* set to a Brandenburg Concerto.

Once in a while, usually late on a Friday afternoon, after an exhausting week of teaching, the beat of Art's pencil was accompanied by very loud humming. The pace would quicken, the pitch would sharpen, and in time Art's humming would fill the corridors and enter the sanctuary known as my office. Then I would hear a few bars from a harmonica, in perfect harmony with Art's loud humming. I soon realized that the harmonica music was coming from the nearby office of Charles Black—a tall, lanky, and somewhat weathered Texan who was a senior member of the constitutional law faculty, famous for his contributions to Thurgood Marshall's brief in *Brown v. Board of Education* and, later, for his eloquent defense of that decision. Art's accompanist was also the co-author of the leading treatise (if you can believe it) on admiralty. A visitor to Black's office was immediately greeted by a panorama of abstract paintings, all his own, and a pile of his poems, mimeographed, waiting for the visitor to take one or two.

All of Art's contributions—the humor, the music, the coffee—were far beyond what we had a right to expect from anyone. They were gifts, gifts of a kind that made the Yale Law School in the mid- and late 1970s such an extraordinary place. During this period the faculty lounge—in truth, Art's kingdom—contained two club chairs, both upholstered in white, facing the door. During faculty workshops and meetings of the governing board, Art was invariably in one of those chairs, usually the one closest to the fireplace. In the years immediately following his death, each time I walked into the lounge I glanced at those chairs and thought about Art and the unique role he had played on the faculty. As years passed, the lounge was redecorated, and the club chairs were finally replaced with a somewhat drab gray couch. An automatic coffeemaker was also installed.

Catharine MacKinnon in May 1989 at the Yale Law School commencement
ceremony. She was a visiting professor at the Law School in 1989 and was chosen
by the graduating students to address them.

8

Catharine
MacKinnon

Feminism in the Classroom

My career unfolded across two worlds. The first, which I entered as a law student in 1961, was defined by a near total absence of women in the profession. The second, which we now inhabit, looks very different: women constitute more than half of law students nationwide and, upon graduation, are able to find positions in all branches of the profession; three Justices of the Supreme Court are women. Catharine MacKinnon—known to many as Kitty—helped me find a path from the first world to the second.

When I attended law school in the early 1960s, Harvard admitted a dozen or so women in a class of five hundred. Erwin Griswold, then the Dean of the Law School and not the type who believed he had done anything he needed to defend, one day acknowledged, over an informal lunch with some of us on *Law Review* (all male), that the small number of women in the class was attributable to a deliberate policy of his. He also went on to explain the reasons for that policy. He thought women seeking admission to the Law School were only looking for husbands and in any event were unlikely to practice law, and so would, in all probability, waste the prized opportunity to study at the Harvard Law School. In response to these statements the students at that luncheon, myself included, said nothing.

During this era the first-year class at the Harvard Law School was divided into four sections, each containing about 125 students, including three or four women. In my first-year section, property was taught by one of the leading scholars of the field, W. Barton Leach. Now and then students volunteered a comment or posed a question, but for the most part Leach conducted his classes by calling on students to recite the facts of a case or answer a question he put to them. At the beginning of the course, though, Leach announced that he would not call on any of the women students on a regular basis. Instead he would designate one or two "Ladies' Days," during which the women students, and only the women students, would be called on. Maybe a few of us chuckled on hearing this, but for the most part we responded to Leach in the same way we responded to Griswold: we said nothing, not a note of disapproval, not even a whimper.

Looking back, I am appalled, as I assume any reader of these pages is, by the practices of Griswold and Leach. Even more, I am ashamed by my silence and that of my fellow classmates. True, we were young, and true, Erwin Griswold and Barton Leach were distinguished figures in a profession we were about to enter. It is also true that, at that time, many educational institutions, including the ones I had attended—Stuyvesant High School, Dartmouth College, and University College, Oxford— were all male. Still, we were living through a great social upheaval, maybe tantamount to a revolution, inspired by a passion for equality—we were the children of *Brown*. How could we—how could I—have remained silent in the face of practices that so grossly offended the principle of equal treatment?

The shameful willingness to tolerate discrimination against women in the early 1960s was not confined to the halls of the Harvard Law School or, for that matter, any law school. It infected all of society. As the bill that was to become the Civil Rights Act of 1964 wound its way through

Congress, Title VII, the section prohibiting employment discrimination, was amended in a way that would link the drive for racial equality with that for sex equality. The amendment added the words "or sex" to the bill so that the statute would prohibit discrimination on the basis of race or sex. Although this amendment would have enormous significance for the future of America, it should be remembered that it was originally designed as a surefire strategy to sink the bill. The sponsor of the amendment, Representative Howard Smith of Virginia, an avid segregationist, could not imagine that in the early 1960s Congress would adopt a measure prohibiting discrimination in employment on the basis of sex. Fortunately, Representative Smith was wrong, though the social forces he was banking on manifested themselves in other ways. During the years I worked in the Civil Rights Division of the Department of Justice (1966–1968), that agency, which was charged with enforcing Title VII, did not bring any suits to enforce the ban on employment discrimination based on sex; neither did it launch any investigations of complaints about sex discrimination.

In time, Title VII became an important tool for rooting out workplace discrimination against women and, as the law changed, so did the academy. By the mid-1970s, when I moved from Chicago to Yale, there were about fifteen women in a class of 165 at the Yale Law School, and Catharine MacKinnon was one of them. After graduating from Smith College, she came to Yale as a graduate student in the Political Science Department. MacKinnon's work in that department was primarily supervised by Robert Dahl, the preeminent theorist of democracy in his day. Soon she made her way to the Law School.

In the early 1970s, Yale launched a new degree program—the Master of Studies in Law—that allowed scholars from other disciplines to study at the Law School for one year. MacKinnon enrolled in that program and, after finishing the year, sought to transfer to the regular JD program. Her application was granted, though only over the objection of some faculty members who argued that such a transfer would be inconsistent with the purposes and rules of the program. I was not a member of the faculty at this time and did not participate in those debates, but as I learned over the years, almost every rule at the Yale Law School has its exceptions.

During my first years at Yale, I offered an advanced course on injunctions that drew on my experience in the Civil Rights Division. Although much of the course was devoted to an analysis of the procedural rules governing civil rights suits, it also provided a forum in which to consider the substantive issues presented by those cases. Catharine MacKinnon was a student in that course. One day she sought me out in my office. Initially, we talked about the tragic death of one of her classmates— some thought it was a suicide—eventually the conversation drifted to legal doctrine.

At that time I was working on an article in which I offered a new interpretation of *Brown* and its edict against Jim Crow (it was published in 1976 as "Groups and the Equal Protection Clause"). The principal wrong of Jim Crow, in my eyes, was not the use of race to make distinctions among people, but the social stratification it produced. What *Brown* condemned, I argued, was any practice, even those that did not make distinctions based on race, that perpetuated the hierarchy among racial groups and that, in particular, subordinated Blacks. As it turned out, Catharine was then writing a paper on the harassment of women in the workplace, a topic of increasing importance as more and more women entered the workforce, and it too focused on the subjugation of disadvantaged groups, in her case women.

The paper Catharine had been working on was being supervised by a colleague of mine, Tom Emerson, a renowned scholar of free speech, who late in his career broadened his interests to the intersection of constitutional law and equality for women. In 1965, Emerson achieved a notable success in *Griswold v. Connecticut*, a case in which he represented the petitioners. In that ruling, the Supreme Court spoke of a constitutional right to privacy and held that it barred a statute prohibiting the use of contraception by married couples. In 1971, shortly before he retired, Emerson and three students (Barbara Brown, Gail Falk, and Ann

Freedman) published in the *Yale Law Journal* a soon-to-become-famous
article on the proposed Equal Rights Amendment. In our initial conversation, Catharine and I talked about her paper (which was eventually
turned into a book and published in 1979 by Yale University Press as
Sexual Harassment of Working Women). We also talked about our mutual
interest in identifying practices that threatened to subordinate disadvantaged groups. Even from this brief meeting, I recognized the tenacity of
MacKinnon's intellect and the depth of her commitments.

Catharine graduated from the Law School in 1977 and then returned
to the Political Science Department to work on her dissertation. She was
still supervised by Robert Dahl, but now my Law School colleague Burke
Marshall joined her committee. As she labored on her dissertation, a
number of important books on feminism appeared, including Dorothy
Dinnerstein's *The Mermaid and the Minotaur* and Carol Gilligan's *In a
Different Voice*. Throughout the late 1970s and early 1980s, it was these
books, along with MacKinnon's on sexual harassment, that most stirred
my students and that were the most frequent subject of their conversations with one another over lunch or coffee.

As interest in feminism grew, I became increasingly troubled by the
absence of any courses on the subject at the Law School. I also had increasingly come to see, in part through Catharine, the vital connection
between *Brown* and the struggle for sex equality. So, in the early 1980s,
I began to offer a seminar, repeated over a number of years, devoted to
feminist legal theory. I acted on the assumption—long part of the folk-
lore of Yale—that the best way to learn a subject was to teach it. Just to
be on the safe side, in putting the course together, I enlisted the help of
another of my students, Reva Siegel, who offered crucial research assistance and who later made her own mark on feminist thought and became
one of my colleagues at the Law School.

The seminar touched on a wide variety of issues: abortion, job protection for pregnant women, government subsidies for child care services,
statutes requiring maternity leave, the evolution of sexual harassment
doctrine, and the theory of comparable work (which attacked the practice

of systematically paying women less than men for work that was of comparable value to a given firm). The most provocative topic, though, was the subject of MacKinnon's PhD dissertation—social practices such as pornography and prostitution, which had, according to MacKinnon, the effect of turning women into sexual objects and in that way perpetuated their subordination. MacKinnon's dissertation was not finished until 1987, but two articles derived from it first appeared in 1982 and 1983 in *Signs*, a prominent journal of social criticism published by the University of Chicago.

In all my years of teaching it is hard to recall any article, book, or judicial decision that provoked classroom debate as intensely as those two articles did. Some of the fire was sparked by MacKinnon's call for the regulation of pornography as part of the feminist agenda, for it seemed in conflict with the Warren Court's protection of art—even sexually explicit art—from government censorship. Even more, the intensity of the class discussion sprang from the suggestion in the *Signs* articles that many women—maybe most women—lack true agency in their sexual encounters with men. This proposition proved incendiary. At one point the discussion became so intense, so free-wheeling, that I and the only male student in the class, Marty Lederman (now a professor at Georgetown), were asked to leave the room. We refused.

Over the next decade, MacKinnon published a series of books—*Feminism Unmodified* in 1987; *Toward a Feminist Theory of the State* in 1989 (her PhD dissertation); and *Only Words* in 1993—elaborating on the themes first announced in her *Signs* articles. MacKinnon's books became a part of my syllabus, and she was also a guest speaker in a number of my courses, including one on free speech that I began teaching in the late 1980s. On one occasion I noticed, upon entering the classroom, an elderly gentleman in the last row who stayed for a good part of Catharine's presentation. It turned out that this man was her father, then a judge on the U.S. Court of Appeals in Washington, D.C., who belonged, some thought, to the conservative wing of that court. In October 1991, Catharine and I spoke on pornography at a conference held at the

Universitá di Roma la Sapienza under the rubric "Women in Civil and Canon Law."

Catharine's lectures were always a vital learning experience for those lucky enough to hear them. She spoke with remarkable power and precision, and she was an inspiring, even charismatic, presence. In my free speech classes the students often sat in awe of her, and I noticed that they were more reluctant than was their custom to challenge the ideas that were being presented to them. Maybe Catharine was the source of this reluctance—she was just too charismatic; maybe I was the problem—I did not manage the occasion in a way that would make the students more comfortable to challenge what she said; or maybe it was the material itself. Arguing that Linda Boreman (more widely known by her stage name, Linda Lovelace) had been coerced into starring in the movie *Deep Throat,* Catharine made a series of bold assertions about female sexual desire and pleasure. Could a large group of twenty-five-year-olds, in mixed company, be reasonably expected to probe those assertions while sitting in room 128 of the Sterling Law Building? Some thirty years ago?

Catharine MacKinnon's work greatly influenced my thinking on issues related to sex equality and free speech. Although pornography was a familiar topic for First Amendment scholars, MacKinnon's theory of objectification cast new light on the subject. Her concern was not with the novels of D. H. Lawrence or even Henry Miller, but with the pornography industry and the bombardment of our culture with images of women that were intended to arouse the sexual desires of men and that had the effect of reducing women to objects to be used by men to satisfy those desires. MacKinnon saw this transformation of women into sexual objects as a threat to the equality of women and Fourteenth Amendment values.

MacKinnon and I also shared a concern about the effect objectification had on First Amendment values or free speech, particularly on the participation of women in public discourse. We both feared that objectification would discourage women from speaking and would undermine their credibility even when they did speak. We feared that in this way the range and force of views available to the public would be distorted. On this assumption, the regulation of the pornography industry might advance rather than endanger liberal values. Although Catharine believed that the Fourteenth Amendment's guarantee of equality could trump the First Amendment's protection of free speech, I primarily saw equality as operating within, and as a part of, the First Amendment.

On one occasion I considered in class an ordinance crafted by Catharine MacKinnon and Andrea Dworkin that sought to curb the pornography industry and the danger it posed to women. In doing so I found myself torn between two former students—MacKinnon and, on the other side, Frank Easterbrook, a student of mine at Chicago who had become a judge on the Seventh Circuit. That court had invalidated the version of the ordinance that had been in effect in Indianapolis, and Easterbrook had written the opinion for the court. The class enjoyed seeing me squirm.

Easterbrook objected to the ordinance on the theory that it was an instance of impermissible viewpoint discrimination. The First Amendment had long been construed to forbid government agencies from regulating speech on the basis of the viewpoint expressed, as, for example, when the chairperson of a town meeting silences a speaker because he or she disagrees with the speaker's opinions. However, the Indianapolis pornography ordinance was not predicated on a disagreement with the views expressed, but on the duty that should govern every fair-minded parliamentarian: to make certain that everyone can be heard. The city council concluded, based on MacKinnon's and Dworkin's work, that the true threat to free speech came from the pornography industry itself, which had silenced women by transforming them into sexual objects. Accordingly, far from reducing free speech, I argued, regulation of the pornography industry should be seen as enhancing it.

Although I found myself drawn to MacKinnon's views about the objectification of women, I took issue with her attack on the objectivity of the law—the claim of the law to be fair and impartial. As a historical matter, MacKinnon's rejection of the objectivity or impartiality of the law was surely accurate. For the most part the received law was a product of a process from which women have long been excluded and as a result might well be viewed, in many instances, as an instrument crafted by men to serve their interests. On the other hand, I felt we should not confuse this historical project of unmasking the received law with a theoretical one that might deny the possibility that law could ever be objective. Indeed, I would go even further and say that, insofar as feminism is presented as a program of legal or constitutional reform seeking to guarantee women equal protection—to extend *Brown* to women—it must presuppose the fairness and impartiality of the law, not just as a theoretical possibility but also as an aspiration. In fact, feminist thought and decisions such as *Planned Parenthood v. Casey*—affirming, in 1992, the rights of reproductive choice first announced in *Roe v. Wade*—reminded large sectors of the bar of the virtue of law as law.

In 1986, I delivered a lecture at Cornell entitled "The Death of the Law?" In it I focused on two movements—Law and Economics, and Critical Legal Studies—that had gained their ascendancy in the 1970s and 1980s. One drew its adherents from the Right and proclaimed that "law is efficiency"; the other drew its adherents from the Left and proclaimed that "law is politics." Despite these differences, both movements, I maintained, denied the capacity of the judiciary to give concrete meaning and expression to the public values embodied in the Constitution and other laws of the United States. I also explained that the ascendancy of these two movements in the 1970s and 1980s arose from a skepticism that had pervaded the academy since the collapse of the Warren Court: We doubted that there were any values that appealed to the public and that were, as in *Brown*, capable of yielding interpretations that were objective and true. In my conclusion, however, I struck a note of hope for the future by pointing to the capacity of the feminist movement and its demand for equality to generate a new appreciation of public values and thus to transform the law into an endeavor worthy of respect and admiration.

In the years since I delivered that lecture the feminist movement has seen ever-increasing successes, so much so that it has in some ways lost its radical edge—it has been normalized. The Yale Law School now has two professors who specialize in feminist thought and also publishes a journal on the subject. Many of the leading cases affirming the rights of women—on a wide range of subjects, including sexual harassment, abortion, employment qualifications, jury service, family leave, and inheritance laws—have been thoroughly integrated into the curriculum. MacKinnon, for her part, is now a professor of law at the University of Michigan and a long-term visiting professor at the Harvard Law School (which since 2003 has had women Deans). In addition to writing and teaching, MacKinnon somehow found the time for an impressive set of practical projects. In one such project she represented a group of women who had been raped by Serbian soldiers during Serbia's invasion of Bosnia. In August 2000 she obtained a judgment by a federal court, acting under the Alien Tort Claims Act, that condemned rape as an instrument of war and that awarded her clients $745 million in damages (though only God knows how that award might be collected). At roughly the same time MacKinnon even managed to publish a casebook, *Sex Equality,* now in its third edition.

We would, however, miss MacKinnon's broader lesson—the need to relentlessly examine familiar practices—if we believed that the feminist project had been completed or if we failed to anticipate the varied and sometimes subtle ways that sex inequalities can arise. No one knows this better than I do. In the fall of 1984, after I had taught the seminar on feminist legal theory for several years, Yale's secretarial and technical workers, predominantly women, went on strike. At the heart of their grievances was a claim of comparable worth: they demanded equal pay for equal work and compared themselves to men working for the University in other departments whose value to Yale was no greater than theirs. Against this backdrop, three students in my first-semester procedure course—Louise Melling, Tanina Rostain, and Catherine Weiss—asked to have lunch with me. I was pleased to accept their invitation, but my mood changed as our luncheon conversation unfolded and I learned that the purpose of the meeting was to complain—about me.

These three students described in painful detail the dynamics in my first-semester procedure class that they felt had the effect of silencing women students: sharp responses by me to some women students; my willingness to recognize students, usually men, who repeatedly volunteered comments in class; my failure to pose questions that might reasonably be expected to elicit a response from women; and a tendency to recognize only the men who happened to cluster around the podium to talk to me after class. Following the luncheon, which did of course have some pleasant moments, I returned to the classroom with their comments very much in mind, but always unsure that I was doing all that I could to foster the equal participation of women in my classes.

In time, two of these students, Catherine Weiss and Louise Melling, expanded their efforts and sought to identify the manifold dynamics that alienated women from legal education. Moving their focus from my procedure course to the rest of the curriculum, they spent many hours talking to their classmates about their personal experiences at the Law School. The results of their inquiries, confirming many of their concerns that led to our lunch in the fall of 1984, were published in 1988 in the *Stanford Law Review* under the title "The Legal Education of Twenty Women."

More than a decade later two other students, Sari Bashi and Maryana Iskander, launched an even more elaborate study of the gender dynamics at the Yale Law School, this time covering the years 2001–2002. The results, published in the 2007 *Yale Journal of Law and Feminism*, indicated that many of the same dynamics persisted. As they wrote, "men continue to dominate class discussion," and "fewer women find faculty mentors and advocates."

We can only hope that today, more than thirty years after the students' grievance about classroom dynamics was first conveyed to me over lunch, things have changed and that the practices that once alienated women from legal education have disappeared. Yet, if I am to be true to MacKinnon's insistent lesson, there may well be reason to doubt that this is the case. There is almost certainly still more to be done, and it is possible that the forces responsible for the alienation lie far beyond the reach of the Law School or, for that matter, any educational institution.

Joseph Goldstein in 1996. He became Sterling Professor Emeritus in 1993, and died in 2000.

9

Joseph
Goldstein

The Scholar as Sovereign

Joe and his wife, Sonja, warmly welcomed me and my family to New Haven in 1974. They were our family away from family. Their friends became our friends. They opened their house to us. They were always available for dinner (Joe would call it a "bite") or for a movie. Joe's father had been in the movie business in Springfield, Massachusetts, and that seemed to entitle him, almost forever, to a free pass to the local multiplex. Joe loved bargains, especially that one. We often talked about our children, and through word and example Joe and Sonja helped Irene and me through our most difficult parenting days. Invariably, they returned from their trips abroad with trinkets for our daughters. Every conversation with Joe ended, "Kiss the girls for me."

Joe was a man of great seriousness of purpose and scholarly achievements. He worked long and hard and was constantly exploring new frontiers and learning new subjects. Yet somehow he always found the time and energy for those he cared about. Joe did not love everyone—no one does, no one can, and besides, Joe was a man of very particular likes and dislikes—but those he loved were among the blessed. They always saw the twinkle in his eyes; they felt the warmth of his presence; they were the objects of his generosity and his extraordinary capacity to go out of his way for others.

Not only did Joe bring a measure of human warmth to the halls of the Yale Law School, which sometimes can be oh-so-serious, but he also espoused a distinctive understanding of the purposes of the Law School. He emphasized its academic as opposed to its professional side, and insisted that its function was not to train lawyers but to study law. Of course, once you study law you may be in a better position to practice it, but that would be merely an incidental (though happy) consequence of the pure, disinterested study of law.

In the late 1970s, Joe began to teach a small group—a class of only seventeen students—the first-year introductory course on constitutional law. He discharged that responsibility in a way that made legal education seem more of a liberal art than a training ground for would-be advocates. His primary purpose was to teach students how to read judicial opinions, and that experience eventually gave rise to his 1992 book *The Intelligible Constitution*.

Years later I discovered that Joe had made special arrangements with the Registrar to make sure the students assigned to his small group were drawn from the first-year section that Guido Calabresi taught on torts and from the one that I taught on procedure. Whatever else may be said about those two courses, they were most assuredly not exercises in professional training narrowly conceived. Joe even refused to follow the trend, then current among small-group instructors, of taking his students to Washington to see the Supreme Court in action or to have the students participate in an end-of-term moot court exercise. Rather than build his class around these more conventional professional activities, Joe sought something greater for his students—an eagerness to approach the law in whatever way would suit their own passions.

To an even greater degree this philosophy shaped Joe's approach to his colleagues. He was extremely demanding, some might say too demanding, in assessing candidates for appointment to the faculty. Yet once new professors were appointed to the faculty, Joe would claim, on their behalf, the same freedom—the same sovereignty—he claimed for himself: the right to pursue their ideas as they saw fit.

Soon after I arrived at Yale in 1974 the faculty met to consider a report from one of its committees on the grading system. By design, the system offered few opportunities for fine gradations: almost all students received a grade of either Pass or Honors. The purpose of the system was to deemphasize grades and prioritize other, more personal assessments of a student's performance. However, in an effort to create new distinctions within the grading scheme, a few instructors had devised a hybrid grade— some called it a "High Pass"—by dividing the credits between Pass and Honors. In a three-unit course, for example, the instructor might give a student one unit of Honors and two of Pass. At this meeting the faculty accepted the committee's proposal to end the hybrid grading practice, despite Joe's deeply felt and strongly worded opposition, which startled those assembled, including myself. Joe regarded the proposed change as a rank interference with the freedom that belonged to every professor to evaluate students as he or she saw fit.

In other contexts, Joe's views about the sovereignty of each individual professor were more persuasive and became, perhaps through Joe's persistent prodding, part of the governing rules of the institution. Joe was especially adamant in defending the norm that the faculty, as a collective, would have no role whatsoever in deciding what or how individual faculty members taught. Professors seeking to offer a new course or to teach an old one in a new way never had to seek the approval of a committee or even of the Dean. Joe was also responsible for the maxim, which I borrowed many times, that it was a professor's job to decide what is educationally desirable and the Dean's to find funds to support this decision. Any other arrangement, Joe feared, would give the Dean the power to curtail scholarly inquiry in the name of budgetary constraints.

Joe's insistence on professorial independence was manifest in many ways, but perhaps most notably in his willingness to cross the conventional boundaries separating the law from other fields of inquiry. After serving in the army during World War II, Joe enrolled at the Yale Law School. Following the first year, he took a leave of absence and entered the PhD program at the London School of Economics (LSE), studying under the tutelage of one of the preeminent political theorists of the twentieth century, Harold Laski. Under Laski, Joe wrote a thesis on organized labor and in 1952 published his dissertation, *The Government of British Trade Unions,* which detailed the breakdown of the democratic processes of the Transport and General Workers Union.

After LSE, Joe resumed his study of law and returned to Yale. Upon graduating, he clerked for David Bazelon, a federal appellate judge who would soon attain fame for his analysis and revision of the insanity defense in criminal cases. Joe taught briefly at Stanford and Harvard and then joined the Yale faculty, teaching in his first years what was then one of the most arid and esoteric of all subjects—bankruptcy. In time, Joe gravitated toward criminal law and family law, and as an extension of his immersion in these subjects (or perhaps his clerkship with Bazelon) he launched a new interdisciplinary venture—law and psychoanalysis.

Joe did not take his interdisciplinary inquiries lightly. While on the Yale faculty he completed a training program at the Western New England Psychoanalytic Institute and became a lay psychoanalyst. In the early 1960s he brought Anna Freud, a prominent English child psychiatrist and, of course, the daughter of Sigmund Freud, to participate in a seminar he was teaching with Jay Katz, a practicing psychiatrist affiliated with the Yale School of Medicine.

Eventually, Yale became the leading center for the interdisciplinary study of law and psychoanalysis. During the late 1970s, Robert Burt (a student in the seminar that Jay Katz and Joe taught in the early 1960s) joined the Law School faculty. When Joe's interests once again shifted to a new field of inquiry, Katz and Burt, each in his own way continued what Joe had begun, carrying forward the tradition of law and psychoanalysis at Yale for the next three decades. That tradition came to an end when Katz and Burt died—Katz in November 2008 and Burt in August 2015—though interdisciplinary studies continued to flourish at the Law School in economics, philosophy, history, political science, sociology, and even psychology.

Joe's work in law and psychoanalysis differed sharply from Katz's and Burt's. He did not use psychoanalysis to underscore the complexities of legal doctrines like "informed consent" that governed the relationship between doctor and patient (as Katz had done). Neither did he see in the psychotherapist a model for understanding the proper role of the judiciary (as Burt had done). Rather, Joe used psychoanalysis as a way of understanding the needs and desires of the people upon whom the law acted, almost as a prelude to reshaping, through the exercise of public reason, the rules that might govern the lives of these people.

Joe's work in this field reached something of a pinnacle in 1973 with the publication of *Beyond the Best Interests of the Child*, written with Anna Freud and another preeminent analyst, Albert Solnit. In that book, Joe and his colleagues, recognizing a child's need for a fully engaged caretaker, advanced the idea of "the psychological parent." They maintained that in custody disputes the claims of such psychological parents should override the claims of biological parents who were not present with the child during its infancy. This view became especially controversial when it was applied to situations in which the child was not abandoned by choice but taken by circumstances, as when Dutch Jews gave their infants to Christian families to spare them from the Holocaust, only to reclaim them years later when they miraculously returned from Nazi death camps.

Not only was Joe a free spirit in his scholarly inquiries, often crossing the conventional boundaries that separated law from other disciplines, but the same iconoclasm governed his teaching. Over the years, the advanced courses Joe offered varied greatly. I marveled at their unconventionality and saw them as an affirmation of Joe's intellectual independence. Quick to deny the authority of the Dean or the faculty as a collective to lord over him, Joe was guided by a strong sense of responsibility to his students and was thoroughly attentive to their needs. He spent endless hours with them, in class and out. In class he always addressed his students as "Mr. This" or "Ms. That," but there was no mistaking the intense personal connection he made with each one. He managed to create that treasured bond between student and teacher, and he earned their devotion and admiration. Joe was also famed for occasionally supervising reading groups, consisting of just a few students, on subjects not covered by the formal curriculum. The weekly meetings of these reading groups took place in his office, or perhaps at a nearby luncheon spot.

Joe also had a very distinctive pedagogic style. He would discuss issues with students, never lecture them. That method worked wonders in small reading groups and first-semester small-group classes. In larger settings, though, especially those outside the walls of the Yale Law School, his method produced certain moments of awkwardness. In 1985 we traveled with our wives to China, accompanied by two of our students, Dan Braverman and Scott Clemens, who spoke Chinese and served as our interpreters. We landed in Shanghai and then journeyed by train for thirty hours to Wuhan, where we were to teach at the university. I gave some talks, or what might pass for lectures, on the *Pentagon Papers* case and, more generally, about free speech. Joe's subject was family law. He stood before the class of about one hundred (wearing, as he always did, a jacket, business shirt, and bow tie). He briefly described the facts of the case, which involved interracial adoptions. Joe identified the legal issue the case posed and then looked out at the sea of students before him, none of whom spoke English, none of whom had ever seen an American law professor, none of whom were familiar with the nuances of American race relations. He waited for some student in the class to say something or to ask a question, and he waited, and waited.

When I arrived at Yale in 1974 stories abounded about how Joe had conducted a disciplinary hearing during the early 1970s, when the University was torn by protests over the Vietnam War and the trial of Black Panthers then being held in New Haven. A sharp exchange in class between a teacher and a Black student led to an after-class encounter in which a classmate of that student allegedly threatened the teacher. Joe was assigned to preside at the hearing but, refusing to assume the posture of a judge, he had the Law School's administration remove the podium and desk at the front of the classroom and replace them with the furniture from his office that he used to meet with students—a couch and some worn easy chairs.

In the late 1980s, Joe feared that the law firm interviewing process was beginning to encroach upon, indeed overwhelm, the intellectual life of the Law School. Students were less worried about the day's lesson than about what law firms were in town or what to wear to the initial, on-campus interview. Visits to law firms for a second round of interviews also drew the students away from classes. With his usual tenacity, Joe spearheaded a campaign to counter these dynamics. Countless memorandums and faculty meetings led to what might have been the Yale Law School's most important contribution to Western civilization—a designated "fly-back week," in which all classes were suspended and students would be interviewed on campus and possibly, if things turned out well, invited to visit the law firm. The hope, and assumption, was that by the end of the week the recruitment process would be over. I am sure that Joe hated the term "fly-back week" to describe this break from classes because it suggests that we might in fact be adjusting the academic calendar to accommodate the professional interests of our students or the demands of law firms—God forbid.

For more than forty years Joe was one of the towering presences in the Law School. Yale took great pride in his scholarly achievements; its fame grew as his did. Even more significantly, Yale bore and still bears the imprint of Joe's distinctive personality and distinctive understanding of its overarching purpose—not just to train lawyers, but also to study the law. He was key in forging the Law School's unique identity. Indeed, it is hard for me to think of Yale without also thinking of Joe, always the gadfly, relentlessly reminding us of the academic mission of the school and the privileges and responsibilities that belong to every teacher. His mark on the institution was so profound and indelible that it almost seems that he is still present—as a knowing smile, as a guiding spirit, and as a conscience. He helped make us what we have become.

Joe died in March 2000, at age seventy-six. Soon after his death my wife and I were having dinner at our home with Sonja and some friends Joe had first brought to the Law School from abroad. One was from Germany, two from Israel. As we sat down for dinner, I offered a toast to welcome everyone and noted how sad and odd it was that Joe—who had first brought all of us together—was not with us. Tears welled up, but Sonja quickly caught herself. "Anyway," she said, "I believe Joe is still watching us."

III
THE FATE OF
THE LAW

Carlos Nino, left, on October 7, 1986, presenting to President Raúl Alfonsín the proposals he had formulated for constitutional reforms to strengthen democratic institutions in Argentina.

10

Carlos
Nino

The Death of a Public Intellectual

In 1976 the military seized power in Argentina and, in the name of maintaining order and combating left-wing terrorism, established a heartless and brutal dictatorship without parallel in Argentine history. This reign of terror included kidnapping, torture, rape, and murder, and led to the death or disappearance of at least nine thousand persons, maybe as many as fifteen thousand, suspected or accused of being terrorists, subversives, or even just left-wing radicals. In the early 1980s, the dictators sought to counter a decline in public support by trying to take the Malvinas Islands from the British by force. They failed in that endeavor and were soon defeated at the hands of Margaret Thatcher. Embarrassed by this turn of events and burdened by a deteriorating economy, the generals who ruled the country decided to relinquish power and call for national elections, assuming that the presidency would be won by the candidate, a Peronist, who promised to leave them alone.

The election was held in October 1983, but to the surprise of many, certainly the generals, the Radical Party candidate, Raúl Alfonsín, won. Alfonsín had campaigned on a promise to bring to justice those responsible for the human rights abuses of the past seven years, and he was true to his word. In the spring of 1985 the leaders of the junta were placed on trial before a civilian tribunal in downtown Buenos Aires. The spectacle that then ensued absorbed all the energy of the nation. It was an extraordinary event in the history of Argentina and, for that matter, the world. It was not the first time that a successor government put the leaders of a previous regime on trial for human rights abuses, but it was one of the very few times that such a feat was attempted without the assistance of a conquering army.

In the midst of that trial, I, along with a small group of lawyers and philosophers from the United States and England (Ronald Dworkin, Thomas Nagel, Thomas Scanlon, and Bernard Williams), was invited by the Alfonsín government to go to Argentina. I immediately accepted and began to prepare for the trip with a certain measure of eagerness, although, to be perfectly frank, I did not have any idea what lay in store for me. I did not know the language, I hadn't a clue about the legal system, and my impressions of Argentine history were based entirely on a quick read of Joseph Page's then-recent book *Perón*. Among close friends I was at a loss to explain the purpose of the trip. I also found it difficult to form a concrete picture of our host and the person who had conceived of this odd academic junket, Carlos Nino. I innocently inquired about Nino from the two I always assumed were most responsible for this extraordinary turn in my life—Thomas Nagel and Samuel Issacharoff (a former student who had spent the previous year in Buenos Aires). They simply described Nino as an adviser to the President.

My own image of a presidential adviser was shaped during the Watergate era. At that time, I was working for the Committee on the Judiciary of the House of Representatives, which was trying to determine whether there were grounds to impeach President Richard Nixon. I spent a great deal of my time during the spring and early summer of 1974 inquiring into the activities of two of the most notorious presidential advisers in American history, John Ehrlichman and Bob Haldeman— dour, cynical opportunists, intensely faithful to Richard Nixon the man, but not to the nation or even to the office of the presidency that they served. Some ten years later, on my first plane ride to Buenos Aires, interrupted by a short stop in Rio, I kept wondering who this adviser to President Alfonsín might be. How far would he fall from the American standard? Little, little did I know.

At our first meeting, Carlos bubbled with conversation. There was a warmth and openness that immediately drew me to him. He was curious about his visitors, attentive to their every need, and always in the best of humor. He loved to tease and joke. He seemed to be the embodiment of life itself. These personal qualities immediately distinguished him from his American counterparts (I will put to one side the chaos and confusion that seemed to emerge spontaneously from his desk). Even more notable was Carlos's love of philosophy. I found in Carlos Nino an adviser to the President who loved ideas—big ideas, abstract ideas, deep ideas, sometimes even strange ideas, but always ideas—and who, in his devotion to speculative thought, distinguished himself from everything American, not just the Ehrlichmans and Haldemans of the world, but even our most honorable officials.

Carlos believed in moral truth. He believed that there were certain principles that were right and others wrong, and that these principles could be used by an individual or a nation in choosing the proper course of conduct. This position was elaborately developed in his book *The Ethics of Human Rights,* first published in Spanish in 1984 and revised and published in English in 1991. Although Carlos's belief in the objectivity of ethical judgments was entirely admirable and much to my liking, it was at times difficult to reconcile this belief with two others that were foundational for him—a belief in deliberative democracy, and a belief in the rule of law. What value can democratic politics have if there is an objective moral truth? The same question could be asked about the law.

Carlos was not the first philosopher who made his career by embracing contradictory propositions. Like the very best, however, he openly confronted the contradictions and tried to reconcile them. He was always so

honest. The result was his epistemic theory of democracy, which assigned a value to democratic politics because it enlarged the range of
interests that would be taken into account in the formulation of public
policy. He pointed to "the difficulty each of us has in representing
vividly the situations and interests of people very different from ourselves" and saw the democratic process as a means of transcending those
limits and achieving a measure of impartiality. For Carlos, democracy
was a surrogate for the informal practice of moral discussion and, in
a fallible world, the best means available for discovering moral truth.
Similarly, he embraced law as a codification of moral truth and gave
it a value insofar, and only insofar, as it was the product of democratic
deliberation.

Theories like this are grist for the classroom and academic journals.
Indeed, Carlos explored these ideas for over a decade in countless articles in academic journals and in one of his final books, *The Constitution
of Deliberative Democracy*. Remarkably, Carlos did not confine these inquiries to the academy. He also pursued them in advising the President.
Carlos conducted his meetings within government as though they were
graduate school seminars—analytically tough, but also speculative and
broadly inquisitive. He assumed that every participant, even the President, had just put down Kant or Kelsen.

During my initial visit to Argentina, Carlos made certain that the visitors from abroad met with the President, and I can remember with great
vividness that first meeting with President Alfonsín. I was struck by the
affection and mutual respect that between Alfonsín and Nino; the President treated Carlos as a beloved son. Even more striking was the scope
of discussion between the two, which ranged broad and far and eventually settled on the work of Joseph Schumpeter, the great political economist who made his career in the first half of the twentieth century. In the
presence of a few interlopers, Nino and Alfonsín sat around a conference
table at the Casa Rosada at this dramatic moment in Argentine history,
speculating about the inadequacies of Schumpeter's theory of democracy.
Perhaps such discussions occurred in the councils of power during the

days of James Madison and Thomas Jefferson. I tried to imagine that kind of conversation occurring within the Oval Office in our time—even in the 1960s—but found myself unable to do so.

While his devotion to philosophy distinguished Carlos from the typical American public servant, his engagement with practical politics distinguished him from most of the world's great academic philosophers. Carlos was not only prepared to address public affairs, which might now be commonplace in the American academy; he was also prepared to act on his theories. Practical politics were an integral part of his effort to make the world just.

When the military seized power, Carlos was not engaged in partisan politics of any type. He was somewhat oblivious to practical affairs and lived wholly in his scholarly world. This did not, however, insulate him from the reach of the dictators, who were prepared to kill those who did no more than espouse unorthodox ideas. As a result, Carlos spent some of the time during the dictatorship living abroad, in England, Venezuela, Mexico, the United States, and Germany. He feared that one day the military would force him to abandon Argentina for good, and that he would have to adopt one of his temporary refuges as "home."

By June 1982, however, the generals began to stumble. They lost the Malvinas War with Great Britain, and as news of the humiliating defeat came to light and the economy continued to deteriorate, unhappiness with the regime grew. Carlos saw a faint opening, and he entered the realm of action, determined to restore democracy to his country. In July 1982, still a year before the junta relinquished power and decided to call for elections, Carlos began meeting informally with a group of lawyers and philosophers who shared his political convictions. This group included some of the most distinguished figures in Argentine intellectual life. Among its members were Genaro Carrió, who later became Chief Justice of Argentina; Eugenio Bulygin, who later became the Dean of the Law Faculty of Universidad de Buenos Aires and a judge on the federal court of appeals; Eduardo Rabossi, a professor of philosophy and the Undersecretary for Human Rights in the Alfonsín administration; Martín Farrell, a noted legal philosopher and judge; and Jaime Malamud Goti, who also served Alfonsín as an adviser and then became Solicitor General of Argentina. Like Carlos, these individuals were committed to restoring democracy to the country and were willing to run all the risks that entailed. Even more remarkably from the perspective of my own cloistered career as a professor, they were also prepared to participate in partisan politics to achieve their purposes.

The first meeting of this group had its difficulties—Carlos had lost the address of where they were to meet and he, along with Eduardo Rabossi, raced up and down Avenida Pueyrredón frantically trying to find the meeting place. From the start, this group turned to the Radical Party, for it had been the traditional bearer of liberal values in Argentina. Still, the members of the group had to decide who, among the contenders for the leadership of the Radical Party, would best serve the democratic cause. They interviewed the various candidates. They made one false start, but felt they had struck solid gold when they were introduced to Raúl Alfonsín. The feeling was reciprocated. President Alfonsín made this group part of his inner circle and affectionately referred to them as "the philosophers." Carlos began his political life as a member of "the philosophers," advising Alfonsín in his quest for the leadership of the Radical Party and, after that was achieved, in his campaign for the presidency. Later Carlos served as the President's adviser on human rights and as the director of a commission devoted to constitutional reform.

For the philosopher king, the field of action is merely a means of actualizing his ideas. For the public intellectual, as Carlos was, the causality flows in both directions. His ideas were shaped by his actions just as his actions were shaped by his ideas. Carlos's intellectual agenda reflected the concrete needs and crises of Argentina; he constantly reformulated and refined his theoretical views in light of lived experience. He spoke to the world, but also was part of it.

In opening oneself to the world in this way, the public intellectual always stands in danger of being corrupted. He can easily put to one side the entrapments of petty politics, or the desire for personal advancement. These never tempted Carlos. The real danger is that the public intellectual might forget the duality of his commitments—that he is committed to the world of abstract thought as well as to the world of action. He may compromise his devotion to the truth in all its fullness because he is eager to get on with the project of which he has become a part. This was Carlos's burden. We talked about it on countless occasions, and it weighed heavily on him.

The great, great public event of Carlos's life was indeed the trial of the leaders of the junta that occurred in downtown Buenos Aires in June 1985, during my initial visit. His involvement in that event left its mark on *Radical Evil on Trial,* a book Carlos wrote with gusto and passion in the months just before his death. One cannot read a page of it without sensing that Carlos was moved in his writing by his profound belief in the justness of the Alfonsín administration's cause and the need to explain the basis of that belief.

The administration's original strategy was to focus on the leaders of the junta. The first prosecution was brought against the nine highest-ranking officers of the dictatorship, and in December 1985 judgment was entered against five of them. In time, the swath of the prosecutions, not fully in the control of the executive, broadened. In the first few months of 1987 there was, partly in response to a new statute that limited the remaining time for new indictments for abuses that occurred during the dictatorship, a sudden surge in the number of prosecutions. By March 1987 more than four hundred officers had been indicted, including many from the lower and middle echelons.

As a result, dissension within the ranks grew, and in April 1987, just before Good Friday, a number of garrisons openly rebelled. Unable to restore order through the ordinary chain of command, on Easter Sunday the President decided, as a last ditch effort, to meet with the rebels in person. He flew by helicopter to the garrison that was at the center of the rebellion. Upon returning Alfonsín declared from the balcony of the Casa Rosada to the multitude assembled below, "The house is in order and there is no bloodshed in Argentina. I ask the people in Plaza de Mayo to leave. And I request of all of you: Go home and kiss your children, and celebrate Easter in Argentina in peace."

No one knows exactly what transpired in the negotiations between the President and the leaders of the rebellious forces. Soon thereafter, however, Alfonsín proposed to Congress a law that would insulate the mid- and lower-level officers from prosecution for many human rights abuses. The intent of the law was to create a presumption that those officers acted in accordance with higher orders and thus, according to Argentine law, were not answerable for their misdeeds. The measure was enacted in June 1987.

Carlos was upset by this turn of events and was unable to hide his disappointment from the President. Carlos's exuberance knew no limits, and my hunch is that he responded to the President's proposal with one of his favorite expressions, "Incredible!" What I know for certain, however, is that the President asked Carlos if his opposition to the measure he was proposing was based on moral grounds. Carlos answered in the negative, and then, very much the teacher, reminded the President that he, Carlos, was not a retributivist. No, Carlos said, his opposition to the new law was based not on retributivist theories of punishment, which he felt would require every single wrongdoer to be punished, but rather on a fear that the new concession would only escalate into an endless series of demands by the military. In that case, Alfonsín replied, the decision was a matter of political smell, and whose sense of smell, the President affectionately inquired of Carlos, should I have followed, yours or mine? Carlos, being true to his beliefs but at the same time trying to define the limits of his involvement with the administration, answered, "Yours, of course. After all, the people elected your nose, not mine."

During the waning years of the Alfonsín administration, Carlos was exhausted from his day-to-day involvement with the business of government. He hungered for the freedom that rightly belonged to him as a professor at the Universidad de Buenos Aires and as a regular visitor at Yale. Yet his commitment to the world of action did not lessen. Outside of government he helped build the Centro de Estudios Institucionales, an independent research institution in Buenos Aires that was to provide a home and base for a new generation of Argentine intellectuals. He also continued to worry about constitutional reform in Argentina and elsewhere.

Carlos died at the end of August 1993, at the age of forty-nine. He was on his way to Bolivia for the second reading of the Constitution that he had helped draft for the country, when, arriving at La Paz airport, so high in the mountains, he suffered a fatal heart attack. On earlier occasions the altitude had bothered him, and he had approached this trip with a certain measure of trepidation. The day after he died, I received from cyberspace this much-delayed message, forcing me to relive his death once again: "Tomorrow I am going for three days to Bolivia. The new deputies need to know what is inside the Constitution because they must decide whether to give to it the necessary second reading. I hope that the highness does not affect much my explanations."

Why, why, Ernesto Garzón Valdés, one of Carlos's mentors, once asked me, trying to make sense of this enormous tragedy, did Carlos go to Bolivia? When Ernesto first posed that question to me in his home in Bonn, I sat in silence. Nothing I could say could adequately respond to the grief we were both feeling. But there can be no doubt about the answer. Carlos was impelled to go to Bolivia, and to Germany, Czechoslovakia, Colombia, and countless other countries, by the same sense of civic obligation that drove him in Argentina, and that soon extended to the entire world.

In August 1994, a year after his death, I was in Buenos Aires once again. Carlos was nowhere, yet he seemed to be everywhere. I cannot be in that magical city for a moment without thinking of him. I could see him in the smiles of his sons, Mariano and Ezequiel. I could see him in the eyes of his wife, Susana, and remembered how deeply he loved his family and how much he enjoyed their times together—in their apartment in the mornings before he walked to his office, in their country house, or on their vacations in Córdoba, Brazil, and even Hamden, Connecticut. I could also see him in the public debates of the day in Argentina.

Politics is the lifeblood of Buenos Aires. Public debate does not await some precipitating event. Yet in July 1994, just weeks before my first visit to Argentina since Carlos's funeral, a bomb had exploded in front of a Jewish organization, not far from where the Centro was located, killing at least a hundred people. The country was once again taking stock of itself. Like me, Carlos was a Sephardic Jew, and soon after we met we became enmeshed in broad-ranging discussions about the role of anti-Semitism in Argentine society. Those early conversations were prompted by Jacobo Timerman's 1981 book *Prisoner without a Name, Cell without a Number,* which described in painful detail Timerman's imprisonment by the junta and the anti-Semitism that seemed to inflame his jailers. Always a believer in the essential goodness of people, and so in love with Argentina, Carlos tended to minimize the presence of anti-Semitism in the country. I wondered what he would say after the bombing.

Anti-Semitism was not the only issue on the public agenda in 1994. As the country tried to recover from the bombing and to make sense of that tragedy, a convention opened in Santa Fe for the purpose of amending the Argentine Constitution. During his presidency Alfonsín pushed for constitutional reform, but was blocked in his efforts by the Peronists. Alfonsín's term came to an end in 1989, and the elections of that year brought to power a Peronist, Carlos Menem, who soon found himself uncomfortable with the restrictions that the Argentine Constitution placed on the presidency. The Constitution provided for a six-year term but no opportunity for immediate reelection. Eager for a second term, in November 1993, shortly after Carlos Nino's death, President Menem pushed for a constitutional convention, and the Radical Party, still headed by Alfonsín, saw this as an opportunity to implement some of the constitutional reforms they had sought earlier. The result was the Santa Fe convention of August 1994.

Carlos had worked hard for constitutional reform, both during the Alfonsín administration and afterward. It was therefore difficult for his family and friends to accept the fact that the convention he had labored so long to bring into being was now being held in his absence. Yet in truth, his ideas were present, and for those who cared to look, Carlos could be seen in the person of Jorge Barraguirre, Gabriel Bouzat, Marcela Rodriguez, Carlos Rosenkrantz, and Agustín Zbar, young people he had trained and inspired at the Universidad de Buenos Aires and the Centro—*los jóvenes*. They had become the advisers to Alfonsín. Now and then, facing some fork in the road, Alfonsín would turn to one of *los jóvenes* and ask wistfully, "I wonder what Carlos would say."

The political battles of the Santa Fe convention were hard fought, and there is no easy way to assess the outcome. The good was often mixed with the bad. Not all would have been to Carlos's liking. Menem got his way, and the Constitution was amended to allow a second term. But in the end there was also a lot of good achieved, and I think it fair to say that those provisions enhancing the protection of human rights, limiting the executive power, and establishing a mechanism to coordinate the work of the executive and legislative branches seemed to vindicate Carlos's vision and to memorialize what he had worked for.

Soon after the close of the convention, I received a letter from President Alfonsín. In it he reminisced about his earlier visits to Yale, while Carlos was teaching there, and praised Carlos for laying the groundwork for the human rights policy of his administration—a policy that he described as one of his "proudest accomplishments." Then the letter ended with this paragraph:

If the Argentine Constitution of 1994 has an intellectual author it is Carlos Nino, who during my government, as Coordinator of the multipartisan Commission for the Consolidation of Democracy, laid the groundwork which permitted those of us who labored in the Constitutional Assembly to come up with most of the ideas and proposals that are enshrined in that document. Carlos was a maker of ideas that worked; his life was too short, but it was also bright, full and good; he is missed.

On my last afternoon in Buenos Aires during the 1994 trip, I returned to El Café de Paso for lunch. It is a restaurant in Parte Once, the Jewish Quarter in Buenos Aires, just a few blocks from the site of the bombing and the former offices of the Centro. The cafe was Carlos's favorite luncheon spot. I had made one of my usual trips to Argentina in August 1993, during which Carlos made certain that we had lunch there before the time came for us to say goodbye. The cafe serves Sephardic food, and we spent hours there eating *bohi'os* and reminiscing about the kitchens of our mothers, and, of course, talking about justice. Two days later I left for Chile and Carlos prepared to leave for Bolivia. On that August day in 1994 when I once again returned to El Café de Paso, Carlos's absence was painful; in saying this I am referring not just to the personal pain, which was greater than words could describe—I came to love Carlos like the brother I never had—but a public pain. There was so much work to do, not just in Argentina, but in all the world.

Although Carlos was not with me, I was not alone. I had brought *los jóvenes* to Carlos's luncheon spot, not just the Argentine *jóvenes,* this time Martín Böhmer and Roberto Saba, but also several Yale students who were there as part of an exchange program Carlos helped establish between Yale and the Centro—Victoria Graff, Julian Kleindorfer, Ken Levit, Janet Levit, and Linda Rottenberg. Having *los jóvenes* with me helped, a lot. Glancing around the table, I realized that Carlos had introduced them to books and ideas that they had never heard of, and that he had broadened their vision in all the ways a teacher should. I knew Carlos would live on through his teaching and the institutions he built and shaped. Carlos had created for himself a unique life, and by his example he had showed *los jóvenes*—no, showed all of us—how we might make our way in this world and perhaps, if the gods are kind, achieve the endearing nobility that he so embodied.

Photograph courtesy of the Yale Law School.

Robert Cover in 1986 at a teach-in on the Yale campus arising from anti-apartheid protests demanding that the University divest from firms doing business in South Africa.

11

Robert
Cover

Cases and Materials

My collaboration with Bob Cover began in the summer of 1974, the year I was moving from Chicago to Yale. No fool, I spent that summer in Washington, D.C., working on the Nixon impeachment. It was Irene who was unloading the crates in New Haven, trying to convince the kids of the wonders of their new hometown, discovering a new pizza restaurant each night, and living in the Covers' third-floor apartment in Davenport College until our house was ready. Bob was teaching at George-town that summer, and one evening I took a break from my work for the Impeachment Inquiry to meet the Covers for ice cream and a walk. Diane, his wife, was with us and graciously feigned some interest in the conversation. Leah was not yet born, but Avi, their young son, was there in his stroller. He made no pretense. He fell asleep the moment Bob and I started talking about what must have seemed the most boring of all subjects: procedure.

The walk was long and directionless. We must have covered every inch of the National Mall. Initially, the conversation focused on the impeach-ment. Our immediate project was to revise the traditional first-year procedure course, and Bob, the true iconoclast, played with the idea of building a new course out of the proceeding then closing in on Richard Nixon. It did not seem to matter to Bob that the presidential impeachment process had not been used for over a century and might well not be used for another. Nor did it seem to matter that an impeachment proceeding is the most rarefied form of legal practice imaginable, professionally involving only a dozen or so lawyers in the entire nation.

We hesitated, however, because we were both suckers for the "great case." Our preferred teaching method was to focus on a single case for a long, long time (some say for an entire semester), using a rich fact situation and a single legal encounter to explore the deepest, hardest issues of the law. At the time of our discussion, the Nixon impeachment had not yet produced that kind of case. The welfare rights movement had, however, so we eventually hit on *Goldberg v. Kelly*, where the Supreme Court found a constitutional right to adversarial, trial-like procedures before welfare benefits could be terminated. With *Goldberg* as our starting point, meta-procedure (as the students named it, to distinguish it from "real" procedure) was born. That was 1974.

Bob died in July 1986 at the age of forty-two. He had a heart attack while driving on I-91, on his way to Boston. Our last conversation, just a few days before his death, was also about procedure. We had changed our meeting place from the National Mall in Washington, D.C., to the streets of New Haven. Bob was wearing his favorite academic attire (at least for the summer)—a T-shirt, blue shorts, and those funny little bicycle shoes. Diane and the kids were not with us this time, but they were very much part of the conversation. Bob seemed to have committed to memory his children Avi and Leah's letters from camp. He relished each detail and had figured out that the closing lines of their letters, "Take me home," simply meant "Don't enjoy yourselves too much." Laughing, we sketched in our minds a *New Yorker* cartoon that would do justice to the kids' ploy.

Bob also spoke of how truly special the past two weeks had been with Diane. Of course he missed the children, but he had been reminded, he said, how much fun it was to be able to go to the movies any night of the week, or to go out to dinner with friends on the spur of the moment—the great indulgences of a modern marriage. Not completely certain whether the kids would consider another summer at camp, he wondered aloud how he and Diane might be able to replicate those two weeks. Drawing on my "vast" experience (my children were just a little older), and having coped with my middle daughter's latest summer adventure, I urged him to place his concerns in perspective. Once his children were tired of camp, they might well decide to spend a summer in Santa Cruz (not at the university, but at the beach enjoying the counterculture festivities).

Bob had a strong sense of priorities and relevance. Diane, Avi, and Leah occupied most of the conversation, and his love for his family informed everything he did and said. But since we had then gotten together to discuss procedure, we managed to spend a few moments on the subject. Judith Resnik had joined our collaboration a few years back, and the three of us were readying a casebook for publication. For the most part this meant shrinking eight thousand pages of material down to about one thousand (although one helpful colleague, knowing full well what editing meant for us, suggested that we could save a lot of time by selling each copy of the book with luggage wheels).

The most plausible candidate for editing was a massive school desegregation case involving New York's Coney Island neighborhood. Over the years, *Coney Island*'s position in the book kept changing, and so did its length. In this draft, *Goldberg v. Kelly* was Chapter 1; *Coney Island*, Chapter 2, had grown to about three hundred pages; and there were five additional chapters. I was, of course, the problem, since I had been long committed to the especially challenging task of trying to convince unsuspecting first-year students that *Coney Island*, despite its extraordinary complexity and procedural innovations, should in fact be viewed as an archetypal lawsuit.

Judith had given up on me. She knew I was hopeless, so she dispatched Bob on the most delicate and difficult of diplomatic missions: to convince me that we should eliminate a sentence, or maybe two, from Judge Jack

Weinstein's *Coney Island* opinion. Of course the change would not put any analytic point in jeopardy, but knowing Bob's weak spot, I pleaded with him: Can you imagine? A generation of law students who know nothing of the "moderating sea breezes of Brighton Beach" or the "fascinating open boat fleet of Sheepshead Bay"? He looked at me sideways, with that knowing, impish smile, and we moved on to other subjects.

No casebook ever served a more sublime purpose. My life with Bob filled the years between these two summer walks, the first in Washington in 1974 and the last in New Haven in July 1986, and it revolved around, of all things, a casebook (eventually published in 1988, having been "slimmed down" to eighteen hundred pages). We were trying to find a way to share with our students the excitement we felt for procedure and, for that matter, the law. The setting of our conversations shifted, from the streets to our offices to the corridors of the Law School to the faculty lounge to Rudy's (for a gourmet lunch of tuna fish and a slice of onion amidst the pinball machines, Pac-Man, and the afternoon television "soaps"). No matter what the place, Bob's brilliance and creativity shone through.

Like all truly creative spirits, Bob played with ideas. He was forever trying out new things, and though some of his ideas were zany (as he would be the first to admit), nearly everything Bob said and wrote startled and amazed me. I was never quite sure when he was going to turn the world upside down (as when, in trying to enlarge the scope of federal habeas corpus rights, he turned "redundancy" into a virtue), or when he would breathe life into tired technicalities (as he did when he envisioned the seemingly dry rules of federal court jurisdiction as "the hermeneutics of jurisdiction"), or when he would make reference to some remote and learned text (like MTV). His ideas were provocative, insightful, totally original. To work with Bob was to experience the special pleasures of being a student again, but with the world's greatest teacher as a friend.

Bob put his ideals into practice. In the early 1960s he was a student at Princeton, but left those sheltered halls to travel to Albany, Georgia, to take part in the civil rights protest occurring there. As a result, he spent three weeks in a Georgia jail. Now and then he would speak of his time with the Student Nonviolent Coordinating Committee (SNCC) in Georgia, but not very often, and then always in a casual, self-deprecating manner. Sometimes a group of students would find out about it and press him for war stories. Others of us might have seized the moment, but Bob demurred, saying he was just a kid then, that many students had been part of the movement, that it was "no big deal." Occasions sometimes arose, however, when he just had to speak out, in class or in print or on the streets, as he did in the early and mid-1980s in support of the Local 34 strike by clerical and technical workers against Yale and in support of the protests demanding divestment from South Africa. Then the depth and intensity of his convictions were apparent to all who listened.

Bob graduated from the Columbia Law School in 1968. He refused to apply for admission to the New York State bar because it required a loyalty oath that offended his deeply held political principles. He also openly opposed the Vietnam War. In joining the Columbia law faculty immediately after his graduation, he was exempt from the draft then in force, but he made his opposition to the war well known. As a young scholar he initially turned to the law of slavery and the abolitionist movement, not as an idle academic exercise but as a way of understanding contemporary judicial responses to draft resistance. His first article was a review of an 1855 book by Richard Hildreth describing the judicial response to slavery, entitled *Atrocious Judges: Lives of Judges Infamous as Tools of Tyrants and Instruments of Oppression.* In 1972, Bob moved to Yale, where his work on the law of slavery culminated in 1975 with the publication of *Justice Accused,* a magisterial study of judges who, despite their apparent moral scruples, put the law at the service of slavery. It won the famed Ames Prize, awarded by Harvard every three years for the best book of legal scholarship.

Bob and I shared similar political values. For us, *Goldberg v. Kelly* was no outlier: it was the culmination of a golden age of American law that had begun with *Brown v. Board of Education.* Indeed, Bob took special pride in an April 5, 1979, *New York Times* op-ed in which he compared a number of the Justices of the Supreme Court to famous baseball players. He compared Earl Warren to Yogi Berra on the theory that, though both were "on teams with many stars," they were "truly the most valuable players." Our shared political commitments were reflected in our decision to build the casebook around *Goldberg v. Kelly* and ignore the subsequent decisions that had rendered that ruling a vestige of another era.

Bob and I were both drawn to procedure because it raised grand theoretical issues in a tough, technical context and for that reason brought to life the law's essential tensions. We also agreed on the aims of the first-year course and the kind of material to which we wished to expose our students. Now and then, we disagreed. Bob not only tolerated and respected such disagreement; he embraced it, for he saw plurality as essential to the human condition. Bob's inclination was always to keep the conversation going, though never by giving in. Indeed, I cannot remember a single instance when he compromised a point or position simply for the sake of going forward (my own "flexibility" is similarly well known). What Bob did do, however, was listen, carefully and patiently, and then build on the ideas we shared. Sometimes, I would think we were at different ends of the earth, but, according to Bob, we weren't all that far apart. Bob brought to these arguments his intellectual gifts, but while he was always dazzling, he was careful never to overwhelm— he gave me room to breathe and to think. Sometimes Bob even went so far as to respond to himself, formulating the argument I wanted to make or should have made in reply. His words were precise, instilled with such integrity and advanced with such gentleness as to turn any argument into a conversation. The initial difference was often resolved, but even when it wasn't, when I turned to leave and walk away, I silently replayed the conversation in my mind and often felt, deep inside, that maybe Bob was right.

Surrender was possible, of course, but with Bob that was a little tricky. In the spring of 1986, when Bob, Judith, and I met in New Haven to go through the casebook a disagreement arose among us over a technical issue involving temporary restraining orders (TROs). This was an area of the law about which I was supposed to know something, and though I tried to ride my authority, both Bob and Judith remained unconvinced. A few weeks later, in the midst of the demonstrations over South Africa on campus, Bob called late one evening to discuss the application for a TRO that was being prepared for students who had been suspended for participating in the protests. He wanted to prevent the suspensions from going into effect. Bob invited me to join the application for the TRO, and as he went over the legal papers that were being drafted, the same technical issue arose again. This time, however, remembering the uneasiness with which I had ended the previous conversation, I had the good sense to surrender: "Anything you decide is fine with me. Just sign my name."

Others would have moved on from there, but not Bob. He seemed a little disappointed. It was late, well after 11 P.M., but he seemed to want to continue the discussion, in a relaxed and casual way, as though we had stumbled upon one another in the corridor early one morning (in most instances that conversation would last the entire day—Bob was the greatest schmoozer in the history of the Yale Law School). On the TRO issue, Bob still thought I was wrong and was quite clear about that, but he knew I attached great importance to the point, and he wanted to make sure I was totally comfortable with the way he resolved it. I promised to review the papers the next morning.

Sometimes our disagreement could not be resolved and went to our fundamentally different outlooks on law. Our political commitments were virtually identical, but we diverged in our understanding of law, or more particularly, on the role of the judiciary. While I saw the judiciary as a tribune of public reason, capable of giving meaning to the highest ideals of the nation, Bob increasingly emphasized its violent nature. In 1983 he was invited to write the foreword to the *Harvard Law Review*'s Supreme Court issue, and the result was his justly famous article "*Nomos* and Narrative." In it he depicted judges, especially those on the Supreme Court, as jurispathic: creating law by killing off the norms that arise organically from tightly woven local communities, so that in the end, only one—the law of the empire—is left standing. When he showed me an early draft of the article I was alarmed and wrote back a short note (leading to endless conversations) expressing my fear that he was betraying the achievements of the Warren Court and the Fifth Circuit—institutions I knew he greatly admired. Judges trying to implement *Brown* sometimes wielded force in the exercise of their contempt power. Yet in my view, such (very rare) acts of coercion or violence could not obscure the essential work of the judiciary and the source of its legitimacy—the reasoned elaboration of our constitutional values.

In debunking the place of reason in the law, Bob's views paralleled those of Critical Legal Studies and its insistence that "law is politics." Bob, however, was not part of that movement; indeed, he was such an original scholar, in both his aspirations and his method of analysis, it is hard to imagine him having belonged to any academic following or ever having wanted any followers of his own. Still, when judges are characterized as jurispathic, and the violent nature of their work is emphasized, the line between law and politics tends to become blurred, or to disappear altogether. His views of the judicial enterprise, like those advanced by the proponents of Critical Legal Studies, was nourished by the disenchantment felt within the academy and in the profession in general when the Warren Court dissolved in the late 1960s and early 1970s and a new majority emerged, determined to eradicate the legacy of the Warren Court and to move the law in an entirely new direction.

In January 1984, Bob and I appeared together on an Association of American Law Schools panel on constitutional interpretation, and I doubt I will ever forget Bob's opening sentence: "Warren Burger is a violent man." In saying this, Bob was making a statement not about the person, but rather about the office that Burger occupied and his exercise of the powers attached to that office. Bob believed that the fifteen years of Supreme Court history that began in the early 1970s—the years of Burger's Chief Justiceship—were utterly deplorable and a fair indication of what could be expected from the judiciary. What was admirable about the Warren Court was not what it said, but what it did: launch a war against Jim Crow; and even this action, in Bob's view, was pro-pelled by "antecedent commitments" that were not in any way gener-ated or constituted by the law. In 1986, Bob published an article in the *Yale Law Journal,* "Violence and the Word," in which he again insisted, with greater intensity than ever, on the law's essentially violent nature.

Shortly after his death in 1986, Diane asked Judith Resnik and me to go through the piles of papers on Bob's desk. In doing so we soon found the handwritten beginnings of a response he was drafting to one of my recent articles, "Out of Eden." In that article I once again paid homage to the reason of the law and extolled the achievements of the Warren Court. I also explained why I felt it was mistaken for Bob to model his understanding of the law on the life of insular religious communities, such as the Mennonites or ancient Hebrews, defined as they were by shared experiences and shared understanding of the good. Focusing on these communities would, I argued, have the effect of slighting or ignoring the generative capacity of law to govern complex multicultural societies like our own. In turn, Bob responded:

I, like Owen, celebrate the achievements of federal courts in de-stroying apartheid in America. Like Owen, I favor federal courts taking a lead in reforming institutions when the other officials fail. But it is Fiss not Cover who is the romantic here. It is Fiss who supposes that these achievements emerge out of a shared community of interpretation that is national in character. I support those efforts because I believe them right and justified, because I am sufficiently committed to them to join with others in imposing our will on those who disagree. At times the federal courts have been our allies in those commitments. There is every reason to believe that such a conver-gence of interests was temporary and accidental; that it is already changing and will soon be a romantic memory of the sublime sixties.

The note was written on a yellow pad, with a remarkably clear and steady hand.

Morton Horwitz teaching a class at the Harvard Law School. The photograph dates from 1978, soon after the publication of *The Transformation of American Law, 1780–1860* and about the time that the Critical Legal Studies movement took shape.

12

Morton Horwitz

Timeless Truths

Morty and I have been friends forever. More than a half-century ago we were high school classmates. We lived in the Bronx—he in Hunts Point, I in Pelham Bay—and we traveled each day on the IRT Lexington Avenue line to Stuyvesant High School, then on East Fifteenth Street and Second Avenue in Manhattan. At that time, Stuyvesant was so over-crowded that it had to operate in shifts. Freshmen and sophomores went to school from noon to 5:30 P.M., while juniors and seniors attended classes from 8:00 A.M. to noon. I cannot recall when, or even how, we first met, but by our junior year Morty and I spent every afternoon together after the day's classes were over.

Typically, we rambled over to a luncheonette on the corner of Fourteenth Street and First Avenue, settled into a booth, ordered a Coke and a plate of french fries, added gobs of ketchup, and spent hours upon hours arguing over issues of economic justice—specifically, whether the state should take from the rich in order to give to the poor. As Morty, only half joking, said when we were both in our seventies and he was introducing me to some of his colleagues, "Owen always sympathized with the ruling elite." The daily lunchtime arguments of our high school years were heated, sometimes very heated. Our quarrels continued on the long train ride home, there was an intermission for dinner, and then in the early part of the evening we picked up where we had left off, using what was then perceived as the greatest of luxuries, the telephone.

We were both from modest backgrounds. His father drove a taxi; mine sold life insurance. His mother was a homemaker; mine sewed in a small garment factory in the neighborhood once my sisters and I were in school, and later worked as a saleswoman at Bloomingdale's. Neither of us had traveled much. I had never been outside the New York metropolitan area, and the same was probably true of Morty. Yet in April 1955, during the spring vacation of our senior year, we, along with a few Stuyvesant friends, embarked on what seemed at the time the boldest of all adventures—a trip to Washington, D.C.

We stayed at the YMCA, ate at what was then probably Washington's only Chinese restaurant, took an evening boat ride down the Potomac, and made the rounds of all the monuments. We also decided to visit the Supreme Court and were together for that extraordinary moment described in Chapter 1, seeing Thurgood Marshall present his argument to the Court in *Brown v. Board of Education*. The particular phase of the court proceeding we witnessed concerned the question of remedy, when Marshall explained why the conflicts that might accompany school desegregation should not be allowed to preclude, or even delay, the remedy that justice required.

After high school Morty and I went our separate ways, though, incredibly, we both wound up teaching law. I studied at Dartmouth, Oxford, and the Harvard Law School. I clerked twice, worked in the Civil Rights Division for two years, and began teaching in 1968 at the University of Chicago, and moved to Yale in 1974. After Stuyvesant, Morty attended City University of New York and then entered the doctoral program in the Government Department at Harvard. After receiving his PhD he decided to study law, also at Harvard, and after graduating he clerked for Spottswood Robinson, a federal appellate judge in Washington, D.C., who had worked for Thurgood Marshall at the NAACP Legal Defense Fund.

During those early years Morty and I managed to stay in touch. We were both students at Harvard when I was in law school and he was working on his doctorate. Morty's clerkship with Spottswood Robinson also overlapped with my work for the Civil Rights Division. We sometimes had lunch, and on one occasion I mentioned that the Harvard Law School had decided to inaugurate a program, intended to honor the recently deceased Mark De Wolfe Howe, to train a new generation of legal historians. I urged Morty to apply, and he did, becoming one of the program's first fellows. After he finished his fellowship Morty was appointed to the Harvard Law School faculty, where he has remained ever since.

Early on, Morty achieved distinction as a legal historian when, in 1978, his book *The Transformation of American Law, 1780–1860* won the coveted Bancroft Prize. As I write in 2016, Morty is at work on an extended history of the Warren Court that, when completed, will be published as part of the history of the Supreme Court, sponsored by the Oliver Wendell Holmes Devise. However, Morty's views on the Warren Court and *Brown* in particular are already clear. For many years he taught a course at Harvard on the Warren Court, and in 1998 he published *The Warren Court and the Pursuit of Justice*. He also dealt at length with *Brown* in his 1993 foreword to the Supreme Court issue of the *Harvard Law Review* in an essay entitled "The Constitution of Change: Legal Fundamentality without Fundamentalism."

Disagreement has been at the core of my friendship with Morty. Our friendship of now more than sixty years has been nourished, rather than threatened, by our disagreements, passionate yet respectful, on issues of great importance. Our disagreement even extends to *Brown v. Board of Education*—the court proceeding we stumbled upon together when we were in high school. Although both Morty and I fully endorse the *Brown* decision, and see it as a transcendent moment in American history, we differ on how it should be understood.

I see *Brown* as law; Morty sees it as a form of politics and, like any political event, as dependent on the fortuities of history and the struggles
for power. Central to Morty's assessment of the *Brown* decision and, for
that matter, the work of the Warren Court in general, is the belief that
Brown constituted a triumph of democracy. He claims that *Brown* sought
to further democracy—to enhance social inclusiveness and to empower
minorities—and, even more, that *Brown* obtains its justification from the
achievement of that purpose. Democracy is, to use Morty's phrase, the
"foundational value" of *Brown*.

Morty believes that this account of *Brown*, emphasizing its democratic
purpose, has a number of advantages. One is that it overcomes an objection, articulated by Alexander Bickel in his seminal work *The Least Dan-
gerous Branch*, to strong exercises of the judicial power because of its
countermajoritarian character. Judges are neither elected nor accountable
to the electorate; and for that reason, Bickel argued, they should be seen
as posing a threat to democracy.

In the years since Bickel wrote, many lawyers have tried to put this
"countermajoritarian difficulty" to rest. Some have emphasized that
America's fundamental commitment is not to pure, unmodified democracy, but to constitutional democracy, which assumes that the decisions
of the majority are constrained by the fundamental values of the Constitution, such as equal treatment under law, and that these values, in turn,
must be protected by the courts, even if the majority opposes them. Others
have defended judicial review against the countermajoritarian objection
by noting that the judiciary often protects, rather than curbs, majoritarian
processes, as when the Supreme Court sets aside restrictions on the right
to vote or other interferences with the electoral process.

Morty takes a different tack altogether. His response, more characteristic of a historian or social scientist than of a lawyer, sees social
inclusiveness as the essence of democracy and treats any judicial decision, *Brown* included, that enhances social inclusiveness as, in and of
itself, furthering democracy and thus not subject to the countermajoritarian objection. As he put it in his 1993 foreword, "The singular

achievement of the Warren Court is that it sought to reconcile the supposed conflict between majority rule and minority rights by assuming that greater social inclusiveness and empowerment of minorities was an extension of democratic values."

The difficulty with Morty's approach can be more easily seen by making a distinction between the procedural and the substantive dimensions of democracy. The decisions of the Warren Court protecting the right to vote and free speech, for example, might be said to belong to the procedural side of democracy: they enhance the capacity of citizens to participate in the processes by which their rulers are chosen and held accountable. The substantive dimension of democracy, in contrast, contemplates enhancing the social position of the disadvantaged or, in Morty's words, "creating greater social inclusiveness."

There are obvious connections between the procedural and substantive dimensions of democracy. At one point Morty speaks of social inclusiveness and minority empowerment as essential prerequisites for the procedures of a well-functioning democracy, as though we cannot have truly open and free elections unless we all stand among each other as equals. Although as a matter of social theory this seems entirely correct, I do not read Morty as intending to instrumentalize social inclusiveness in this way. He would acknowledge that social inclusiveness may be necessary for free elections, but he also moves beyond that point. When he insists that democracy is the foundational value of *Brown*, not just of the Warren Court's election or free speech decisions, Morty is primarily treating democracy, understood in its substantive guise, as an independent value in and of itself.

Those who complained about the countermajoritarian character of *Brown* were complaining about the Court's interference with the procedural component of democracy; they were objecting to the decision of the judiciary to set aside a mandate from the majority of voters. Of course, in response, one might point to the disenfranchisement of Blacks and their exclusion from the electoral process and justify the refusal of the judiciary to heed the decisions of the political branches. Many have defended

Brown on such a theory, and in that way have overcome the countermajoritarian difficulty.

There are situations, however, in which the countermajoritarian difficulty cannot be elided in this manner. In such cases the requirements
of democracy, understood in a procedural sense, might be fully respected,
and yet the majority may nonetheless end up oppressively disadvantaging
the minority. Imagine, for example, a situation in which a legislative majority, acting freely and with full information, and in a system in which
all racial, ethic, and religious minorities enjoy full and robust voting
rights, enacts restrictive or illiberal policies that disadvantage a racial minority. Morty might object to such enactments on the ground that they
interfere with democracy as substantively understood (that is, as requiring
social inclusiveness or minority empowerment). Such an account, however, would have to confront afresh the countermajoritarian difficulty,
for judicial intervention aimed at protecting a racial minority would be in
serious tension with the procedural understanding of democracy. In a
sense, democracy would be on both sides of the balance.

For this reason, talk about democracy *simpliciter* or to characterize
Brown or the work of the Warren Court in general as "an extension of
democratic values" will not resolve the dilemma posed by judicial review.
The justification for judicial review can be found only in an understanding
of the United States as a constitutional democracy and in an appreciation
of the role of the judiciary, as a nonmajoritarian institution, to vindicate constitutional principles, including the guarantee of equal protection.
In sum, the emphasis on the social empowerment achieved by *Brown*
is both unneeded and, in the final analysis, less than fully effective in
responding to the so-called countermajoritarian objection to judicial
review.

Wholly apart from its significance for overcoming the countermajoritarian difficulty, Morty's decision to identify democracy as the foundational value of *Brown* enables him to embrace the idea of a "living constitution" and to develop a theory of legal change that avoids the pitfalls of
what he perceives to be a static jurisprudence. He believes that once de-

mocracy is seen as lying at the heart of *Brown* he is able to justify the repudiation of the 1896 *Plessy v. Ferguson* decision and its "separate but equal" doctrine, and to do so in far more radical terms than permitted by the views of most lawyers.

The standard account treats *Plessy* as an error, a mistake later to be corrected by *Brown*. This view assumes the *Plessy* Court in 1896 either misunderstood the social meaning of racial segregation or misconstrued the purposes of the Fourteenth Amendment. Morty asks us to imagine, however, that *Plessy* might have been right at the time it was decided, just as *Brown* was right when it was decided. How can this be, if between 1896 and 1954 there was no amendment under Article V and there was, in Morty's view, no change in the underlying facts or even in our understanding of those facts? Once democracy, in the substantive fashion in which he understands that term, is seen as the foundational value of *Brown*, Morty believes he can explain the shift between *Plessy* and *Brown* in terms of the changes that occurred in the nation's values between 1896 and 1954, for it was only during that period that democracy, in the full sense of the term, achieved, in the political domain, its authoritative status.

According to Morty, democracy was not perceived as fundamental in the constitutional discourse of the nineteenth century. It achieved its ascendance in the early twentieth century thanks to contingent political events: the rise of totalitarianism, the horrors of World War II, the struggle against the Soviet Union during the Cold War. Surveying these developments, Morty urges us to see *Brown* not as a correction of an earlier mistake, not as the expression of a timeless truth, but as a generous and noble vindication of a newly triumphant value, democracy.

Despite the characterization of democracy as a fundamental value, and even more as *the* foundational value vindicated by *Brown*, it is important to note that Morty is unwilling to treat it as a value embodied in the Constitution. Democracy may be the prism through which modern Justices see and understand the Constitution. It guides them in their decisions and interpretations but is not something whose authority is derived from the fact that it is, in any ordinary sense, inscribed in the Constitution or implied by it.

In his 1993 foreword Morty declared that, in treating democracy as the fundamental value implemented by *Brown*, he was offering an account of "fundamentality without fundamentalism." The fundamentalism that he sought to avoid is known as originalism, but it might properly be called intentionalism because it holds that constitutional interpretation should be governed by what the framers intended. According to this school, the first question that the Court should ask is whether the framers of the Fourteenth Amendment intended to outlaw racial segregation. If there is no settled intention on that issue because, for example, the practice was not widespread in 1868 and thus not central to the deliberations of the framers, the Court should then try to ascertain what the framers would have thought about the practice.

Morty rejects this form of originalism, and he is entirely right in doing so. It is difficult to ascertain what the intention of the framers regarding some specific practice was or might have been. Even more important, intentionalism is inconsistent with the very nature of a constitution seen, as it was by the framers, as a public act; one that would, upon promulgation, take on a life of its own; one whose meaning belongs to those generations who would be governed by it. Yet to reject the intentionalist form of originalism, as one should, does not require one to accept the idea of a "living constitution," or to reject all types of originalism. Rather, there is a form of originalism—similar to the conception of purposivism advanced by Aharon Barak in his 2005 book—that is not subject to the objections voiced against intentionalism.

For purposivists, the Constitution is an embodiment of public values, and the judiciary is charged with the task of giving these values concrete meaning in the life of the nation. The emphasis is not on the intentions of the framers, although they may enter into the equation, but rather on the general purposes of the constitutional provision at issue. The judge identifies the purpose by looking at history, text, and structure, and from this understanding constructs the principles that guide his or her interpretation. Of course, for the purposivists, democracy may be treated as one of the values embodied in the Constitution that is to be given concrete meaning by the judiciary—indeed its chief value, if we are to believe Justice Stephen Breyer, who has written extensively on "Our Democratic Constitution." Yet Morty does not treat it that way. For him, as I have said, democracy is not a value embodied, enshrined, or determined by the Constitution; it is a political accretion that has gained authority by a series of fortuitous political events.

In the name of modernism, Morty denies that there are any values rooted in or authorized by the Constitution that have a force independent of how they are interpreted. Yet for someone who believes that democracy is the foundational value of *Brown*, as Morty does, this modernist perspective cannot stand as an objection to purposivism. The values that I see embodied in the Constitution and that serve as the predicate of *Brown*, values such as racial equality, are not, as a philosophical matter, different in kind from democracy. Both need to be interpreted; both always come to us already interpreted. The only difference is that one type of fundamental value gains its authority from the processes of constitution-making, the other from ordinary politics or the long, highly contingent course of history.

Purposivism might be viewed as a form of originalism, or even fundamentalism, not because it permits some reference to the intention of the framers, but because it presupposes that, absent recourse to Article V, the principles of the Constitution do not change. Facts change, applications of principles change, but the principles themselves remain unchanged. The social milieu in which the judiciary operates also changes, and that change will inevitably influence the judiciary's understanding of the principle to be applied. But the Justices' job is to divorce themselves, as best they can, from such circumstances. They should strive to articulate a meaning of the Constitution that is true for all time, subject to correction by those who follow, provided the successors can show that the earlier Court applied the wrong principle or applied the right principle wrongly.

Morty rejects the intentionalist form of originalism, in part because it inevitably puts the law out of touch with social reality. Even though purposivism may be seen as a form of originalism, it is not vulnerable to the same criticism. The governing principle, assuming it is the correct one, may remain the same, but the Court is charged with the duty of taking account of new social realities when it applies that principle. As Chief Justice Warren explained in *Brown* itself, in order to finesse *Plessy* it was incumbent on the Court, in applying the Fourteenth Amendment, to take account of the changes that occurred in public education over the course of the twentieth century.

Morty's theory of fundamentality is more accommodating of change than purposivism is. Morty contemplates both that social reality will change and that the principles to be applied will themselves change. Although Morty gives us no detailed account of how a value such as democracy acquires its authoritative status, surely it entails a long, arduous process with deep historical roots. Yet an element of flexibility or adaptability is introduced by his account of fundamentality since there is no need to show that the principle or fundamental value is part of, or embodied in, the Constitution as written in 1787 or as amended. It is difficult, however, to know what to make of this feature of Morty's theory because it is hard to identify the right degree of flexibility. In the end, Morty's "living constitution" just might be too much in flux or too changeable because it is inconsistent with the most elemental understanding of constitutionalism, an ideal that necessarily implies, at least at the level of principle, a strong measure of fixity.

Ultimately, I suspect that what divides Morty and myself is not so much a difference in our attitudes toward the optimum amount of flexibility, or the amount of flexibility consistent with the ideal of constitutionalism, but rather our divergent outlook, traceable to the very roots of our friendship, on the legal profession and law in general. Morty, one of the founders of Critical Legal Studies (CLS), has always stood outside the law and sought to unmask it, determined to erase the line between law and politics. Several years ago, at a banquet in Morty's honor, Duncan Kennedy, another founder of CLS, no longer an enfant terrible but more a seasoned elder statesman, spoke with fond memories of his conspiratorial activities with Morty during the late 1970s and 1980s. At that time the two conferred over the phone almost every evening to formulate their plans for wreaking havoc on the established ways of the Harvard Law School, which was once, at least during my student days, a bastion of conservatism. In Kennedy's telling, it was as though the conflicts that the two were hoping to engender over faculty appointments or the grading system were to be the opening salvos of The Revolution.

CLS never took hold at Yale, or perhaps to put it more cynically, was not allowed to take hold there, certainly not in its most virulent form. I joined the Yale faculty soon after many of the young, more radical professors were let go. During my tenure Yale became the home of what was generally, though not entirely with affection, referred to as "central liberalism." Those whose views were so categorized, like me, believed in the law. Morty and I have been friends forever, but he is a radical and I am not. I work from the inside out, searching for virtue in the legal craft. Perhaps this search of mine can be brushed off, as Morty once characterized it, as reflecting nothing more than my sympathy for the ruling elite. I would like, however, to believe that another instinct is at work.

I have been guided by the hope that a discourse that locates fundamental values in the Constitution and that puts the judiciary to the task of articulating those principles that will govern for all time will both discipline the Justices and give us a set of standards that can be used to evaluate their performance. In fact, this is what we saw, or at least I saw, in Washington in April 1955—not a free-floating idealism, but rather a studied attempt to use the ways of the law to realize the idealistic possibilities of the Constitution.

Aharon Barak in late 2006, shortly after stepping down as President of Israel's Supreme Court.

13

Aharon
Barak

Law Is Everywhere

Aharon Barak was born in Lithuania in 1936. During World War II
the Nazis occupied the town in which he lived, and in the final months of
the war they introduced an especially brutal dimension to the inhu-
manity of their rule. They decided to exterminate all of the Jews younger
than twelve, on the theory that they were, in the phrase later used in the
Holocaust encyclopedia, "useless eaters." At that time, Aharon was eight.
His parents managed secretly to get him out of the ghetto. For the next
six months he and his mother hid in the walls of a neighbor's house, while
his father, once a lawyer, continued to labor in the ghetto. At the end of
the war Aharon and his parents traveled across Europe, from one refugee
camp to another, eventually making their way to Israel.

In time, Aharon Barak became a professor of law at Hebrew University and later served as the Dean of the Law Faculty. Then, from 1975 to
1978, he was the Attorney General of Israel. In 1978, shortly before he
turned forty-two, Barak was appointed to the Israeli Supreme Court,
though he was almost immediately granted special dispensation to serve
as Prime Minister Menachem Begin's legal adviser at the Camp David

peace talks, held in September of that year. In 1995, Barak became President of the Supreme Court of Israel, a position he held until his retirement in 2006.

Nowhere is Barak's legacy more formidable than on issues of national security arising from terrorist attacks on Israel. Although his rulings in this domain have long been heralded throughout the world, they acquired new meaning and cogency for us on September 11, 2001. On that day, terrorists, operating under the direction of al-Qaeda, attacked prominent sites in the United States, resulting in enormous destruction of property and the death of more than three thousand people. In response, the United States launched the War on Terror, which continues to this day.

The War on Terror began as a military operation against al-Qaeda, but over the last fifteen years, it has become a sprawling, never-ending armed foray into distant lands, mostly in the Middle East. Soon after the initial attack on al-Qaeda, we invaded Afghanistan, then ruled by another radical Islamic group, the Taliban, for harboring and sheltering al-Qaeda. In March 2003, the United States invaded Iraq, not because it was in any way responsible for the events of September 11 or had any tie to al-Qaeda, but to overthrow Saddam Hussein on the theory (later proved false) that he possessed weapons of mass destruction and thus posed a threat to the United States and its allies. Nevertheless, Iraq became another site of the War on Terror when terrorist attacks, sometimes led by al-Qaeda or an affiliate, were directed against the United States' forces occupying that country. The War on Terror was further enlarged when the President of the United States decided to treat a number of terrorist organizations, all claiming to follow the creed of Islam, as "associated forces" or "allies" or "co-belligerents" of al-Qaeda: al-Qaeda in Iraq; al-Qaeda in the Arabian Peninsula (based in Yemen); al-Shabaab (in Somalia); and most recently the Islamic State in Syria and Iraq (ISIS).

The War on Terror was announced by President George W. Bush and continued through the end of his years in the White House. In the 2008 presidential campaign, Barack Obama promised change, but once elected continued the war with the same determination. Some of Bush's ways of fighting were discontinued; others were expanded. Obama refused to use the term "War on Terror" but repeatedly insisted—even after Osama Bin Laden was killed in May 2011 in his compound in Pakistan—that the United States is at war with al-Qaeda and its associated forces.

Both presidents, one a Republican and the other a Democrat, have fought the War on Terror with the determination you would expect of a Commander in Chief—wars are always fought to be won. Unfortunately, this resolve has led, usually with the eager endorsement of Congress, to the institution of practices that transgressed long-honored limits on the exercise of executive power: the use of torture in interrogations; targeted killings of suspected terrorists; prolonged, indefinite detention without trial; the use of military commissions; warrantless wiretapping and electronic surveillance of civilians on a massive scale; and the criminal prosecution of political advocacy deemed to support designated foreign terrorist groups.

Since they were instituted, these practices have been the subject of a great many lawsuits aimed at protecting the Bill of Rights or seeking to hold the executive accountable for its abuses of the law. For the most part, however, these suits have not been successful. Sometimes petitioners have been denied access to the courts altogether. Many more returned empty-handed because judges deferred to the political branches. A few prevailed but obtained only the most limited relief. Collectively, these rulings stand as an indictment of the American judiciary, long viewed as a paragon of liberalism. They also make the achievements of Aharon Barak all the more remarkable. Not only did Barak hold the Israeli government in its fight against terrorism accountable to the law and thus protect basic liberties, but he did so even when the threat of terrorism was greater than that the United States faced since the terror attacks of 2001.

We have had the benefit of geographic distance. The terrorist organizations that have threatened the United States are based in foreign lands. It may be that al-Qaeda and its so-called associated forces have agents within the United States, but their nerve center is located half a world away, in the Middle East. Israel's enemies, such as Syria and Iran, are its neighbors, and terrorist organizations have their centers on Israel's borders—for example, Hezbollah in Lebanon and Hamas in Gaza.

The specific terrorist attacks that Barak encountered while on the bench—suicide bombings and the rockets of Hezbollah and Hamas—may not have had the same ghastly quality of spectacle as the September 11 terrorist attacks, but they were more pervasive and wrought death and destruction on an enormous scale, especially given the small size of the country. In Israel the threat of terrorism that Barak confronted was woven into the fabric of everyday life.

Some of the atrocities that Israel encountered have been fueled by the same kind of inchoate hatred that impels al-Qaeda. Other attacks on Israel may have been motivated by a discrete strategic objective: to replace the Israeli occupation of the territories it acquired in the 1967 War with a new Palestinian state; these might be similar to the terrorist attacks targeting American forces occupying Iraq and Afghanistan. For the most part, however, the terrorist attacks against Israel pose an existential threat to the country—to "push the Jews into the sea." The attacks of al-Qaeda on the United States on September 11 cannot plausibly be regarded as having such grandiose ambitions; neither can any of the sporadic terrorist attacks or attempted attacks against the United States that have occurred since 2001.

Barak's rulings in defense of basic liberties were all the more remarkable because Israel has no written constitution, and thus any claim of right against the political branches must rest on more elusive sources. At the time of Israel's founding in 1948, plans were made for the formulation and adoption of a formal, written constitution. In fact, Israel's Declaration of Independence promised that a constitution would be adopted no later than October 1, 1948. But those plans never came to fruition. So Barak, following in the tradition of his predecessors, constructed many of the governing principles of Israel—its body of constitutional law—as an elaboration of Israel's foundational aspiration to be a free and democratic society, as set forth in its Declaration of Independence. He was required, in his words, to build "constitutional law without a constitution."

To be sure, Barak had some formal legal sources to rely on, including statutes of near-constitutional standing. Once the plan to adopt a written constitution failed, the Knesset (the Israeli parliament) began enacting a series of statutes known as the Basic Laws, which purport to set forth the governing principles of Israeli society. For Israel's first forty years, the Basic Laws primarily addressed the structure and organization of government powers. In 1992, however, the Knesset took a new turn and adopted a Basic Law guaranteeing human dignity and freedom.

The 1992 Basic Law can properly be seen as part of the human rights tradition, and it resembles the United States Bill of Rights in both the generosity of its spirit and the generality of its language. It has functioned for Justice Barak much as a written constitution, with one important exception: the supremacy of the legislature—a key feature of Israel's parliamentary system—is preserved. This means the Knesset could, at least in theory, unmake its guarantees almost as readily as it made them. Thus most Basic Laws, including the one on human dignity, can be amended by a simple majority of those present.

Israel is a small country of around eight million people, covering an area roughly the size of New Jersey. The country's political culture is characterized by spirited public discussion (to understate the matter). Barak's rulings were widely known to the electorate in Israel and they have always been the subject of great controversy. Some attempts have even been made to overturn them. In one notable instance Israel's Minister of Justice proposed amending the Basic Law on human dignity in order to reverse one of Barak's decisions. The ruling—one of Barak's last—struck down a statute exempting the state from compensating Palestinians in parts of the occupied territories for injuries caused by Israeli security forces. That law had applied to all such injuries, whether or not they were related to legitimate military operations. In the course of his career on the bench, though, none of these efforts succeeded, which is a testament both to Barak's decisions and to the strength of the country's foundational commitments.

Barak's constitution is one without borders. It binds Israeli officials wherever they might be, and it protects citizens and noncitizens alike. Its overarching aim is to protect human dignity, which Barak sees as the foundation of democracy; and it is the source of the rights all people are owed by virtue of their humanity. The depth of this commitment was most clearly revealed in his decision denying the military the authority to subject anyone, even suspected members of Hamas or Hezbollah, to harsh and aggressive interrogation techniques properly regarded as torture. Impelled by respect for the dignity of all persons, he fashioned a prohibition of torture as absolute as the one found—at least before September 11, 2001—in the United States Constitution.

Some commentators have questioned the absolute nature of this prohibition by imagining a scenario in which the only way to avoid a great loss of life is by torturing a prisoner. In this scenario, a bomb of enormous power is ticking away in a city and only the prisoner knows where it is located. In his ruling limiting aggressive or coercive interrogation techniques, Barak confronted this dilemma, even though the facts before him did not require him to do so, and he held that even in so dire a context prior authorization of torture would be unconstitutional. The offense to human dignity would be too gross.

Barak acknowledged that the guard who tortured the prisoner in this hypothetical scenario might be able to assert, at a criminal trial after the fact, the defense of necessity; and on that ground he might—only might—be exonerated. On principle, some have criticized Barak for this concession. Yet this critique must be tempered by the realization that even the most absolute of rules can be subject to exceptions in their application. For example, even under U.S. law, someone who tortured a prisoner to save innocent lives or to prevent the destruction of a city could assert, in a criminal prosecution brought against him, a necessity defense; or more likely, he could trust a sympathetic jury to nullify the law by reaching a verdict of not guilty.

For the most part, though, Justice Barak's principles are not absolutes like the prohibition of torture; instead they seek an accommodation of conflicting values or, as he has put it, "clashing considerations." In that sense they are like the Fifth Amendment's requirement of "due process" or the Fourth Amendment's protection against "unreasonable" searches. The words "due" and "unreasonable" necessarily entail a consideration of conflicting values. As a result, the liberties these amendments protect are especially vulnerable in times of national stress, when military necessity is often said to justify a sacrifice of individual freedom. For that reason, Barak's work is especially admirable because he has sought to create a distinctive judicial method—call it a jurisprudence—that acknowledges military necessity without allowing it to overwhelm the freedom that dignity requires.

This method accounts for two of Barak's most important rulings on terrorism. One required the Israeli military to reroute the security fence that it was building between itself and the occupied territories to prevent the infiltration of suicide bombers and other terrorists. The other, announced in the so-called targeted-killing case, limited the power of the military to kill persons who are civilians but who are suspected by the military of engaging in terrorist activities.

Like any good judge, Barak began his analysis in these cases by acknowledging the values—all the values—at stake in the controversy. He recognized the interest served by the government's action, as well as the harms that would likely be inflicted by the proposed action. He accepted that national security—the survival of the nation and the protection of Israeli lives—was a compelling justification for government action. But he also maintained that respect for human rights and human dignity were pillars of democracy, not to be casually cast aside.

Although many jurists have faced similar dilemmas, Barak's distinctive contribution was to place limits on the deference due to the military. In his opinions he drew a sharp distinction between the assessment of military needs and the question of whether a military action is normatively justified given its impact on fundamental values. On the question of military needs he was prepared to defer to the government's assessments. Yet he saw it as the essence of the judicial role to determine whether the pursuit of those needs unjustifiably interfered with the exercise of a protected liberty or a fundamental value.

In the security fence case, for example, those objecting to the route of the fence offered evidence—the testimony of experts with considerable military experience—to show how military needs could be satisfied by building the fence along a line other than the one proposed. Yet Barak was not prepared to second-guess Israel's armed forces on that score, and accordingly saw the military's initial judgment on how to satisfy security needs as determinative. He took this view not because of the military's expertise on issues of national security, but because the military alone is responsible for the technical quality of its actions. By contrast, Barak reserved for the judiciary the function of determining whether an infringement of basic rights would be so great as to bar the military from acting as it wished. There was to be no deference in the realm of values. That judgment, in his view, belonged to the judiciary.

The American judiciary has a strong tradition—especially salient in the post-9/11 era—of judicial deference to military authorities. To date, though, we have failed to make Barak's distinction. The deference of the American judiciary goes to the military's assessment of the technical needs of national security, as well as to the question of whether, given the harm to fundamental values, the military's action is normatively justified. By granting the executive wide latitude in both the choice of how to pursue its objectives and in the normative determination that the gains to be achieved by its action outweigh the loss to basic freedoms, U.S. courts allow the executive alone to strike the balance between military needs and core values. Such blanket deference is deeply troubling.

Admittedly, in a presidential system like that of the United States, the executive and the legislature have independent sources of legitimacy. In theory, this could allow Congress to act as a check on the President. Yet, as the enactment of the Detainee Treatment Act of 2005, the Military Commissions Acts of 2006 and 2009, and the 2008 amendments of the Foreign Intelligence Surveillance Act (FISA) illustrate, in the face of terrorism the legislature is, as often as not, complicit in the transgression of basic liberties. Thus, blanket judicial deference to the executive in national security matters is no more justified in a presidential system than in Israel's parliamentary system. In both, the judiciary must act to preserve constitutional values and thus rigorously scrutinize the tradeoff proposed by the executive between freedom and security.

Sadly, the American judiciary has proven unequal to this task. In 2004 the Supreme Court held in a case involving an American citizen that, as a matter of due process, a person imprisoned as an enemy combatant had a right to an evidentiary hearing on the claim that he had not taken up arms against the United States. However, Justice Sandra Day O'Connor, the author of the Court's opinion, was explicit in calling for deference to the military in making this determination. She was willing to assign to prisoners the burden of proving that military field records were mistaken. She was also willing to allow "properly constituted" military tribunals—not civilian courts—to decide the merits of each claim.

Similar deference explains the failure of U.S. courts confronted with the excesses of the War on Terror to require that the government charge with a crime and bring to trial enemy combatants held for prolonged, indefinite periods of time. It also explains the American judiciary's failure to offer redress to victims of extraordinary rendition and torture (indeed, its refusal to even inquire into the merits of allegations of torture). I also suspect that fear of interfering with the executive's capacity to conduct foreign affairs or protect national security could also explain the Supreme Court's 2013 decision denying journalists, lawyers, and human rights researchers standing to challenge the 2008 FISA amendments that vastly expanded the scope of warrantless wiretapping.

Barak rejected this kind of blanket deference as a dereliction of judicial duty. He also identified, with greater clarity than any American jurist, the appropriate inquiries to determine whether a government action that restricts basic freedoms can be justified. This set of inquiries, which he refers to as the "proportionality test," examines both the instrumental and the substantive rationality of the government's action. Justice Barak pursued these inquiries in all manner of cases, but they had their greatest force in his rulings on national security.

The first part of the proportionality test, the instrumental inquiry, concerns the relationship between means and ends: it asks whether the means the government has chosen in pursuing its policies are rationally related to its ends, and more important, whether the chosen means are the least restrictive alternative. The means must be narrowly tailored to achieve their purpose, fitting, to use Barak's metaphor, as closely as a suit might fit a body. In other words, the sacrifice of fundamental rights must, according to Barak, be kept to an absolute minimum. If the government has an alternative way of meeting its needs that entails less of a sacrifice in these rights, the original course of action cannot be permitted.

In the targeted killings case, for example, Barak fully appreciated the danger of terrorist attacks, yet he sought to carefully cabin the power of the military to assassinate suspected terrorists. He drew a sharp line between enemy combatants and civilians and was wary of placing civilians who were suspected of terrorism in yet a third category—that of unlawful combatants—that would afford neither the protections given to combatants nor those given to civilians. Although the laws of war allow the military to kill combatants in an active theater of armed conflict, civilians can never be targeted, though they may be killed as so-called "collateral damage." Civilians may forfeit this protection and be targeted only when they participate in hostilities, such as terrorist attacks, and Justice Barak stringently defined the conditions for such forfeiture. Links to or membership in a terrorist organization would not, by themselves, be sufficient. Instead, the person targeted must have taken a direct part in hostilities and could only be permissibly targeted while engaging in such hostilities. Even then, the military could not target the suspected terrorist so long as capture and trial were feasible. As Barak reasoned, "among the military means, one must choose the means whose harm to the human rights of the harmed person is smallest."

In an analogous context, the U.S. Supreme Court, under the rubric of strict scrutiny, has required that when a fundamental value like free speech or racial equality is threatened the government must use the least restrictive means available to pursue its end; or, to use another formulation, governmental interference with a privileged value must be no greater than necessary. Unfortunately, though, the Court has applied strict scrutiny only intermittently, and hardly ever in the context of war. Perhaps most infamously, the Supreme Court did not insist on the least restrictive means or least harmful alternative in *Korematsu v. United States*. In that 1944 decision the Court gave constitutional legitimacy to the mass relocation of persons of Japanese ancestry living in the western states during World War II. Although the Court said that it was applying, in its own terms, "most rigid scrutiny" to the relocation program, it nevertheless deferred to the government's assessment of the need for such a policy, and more important, it never considered whether less harmful alternatives were available.

The second type of inquiry in Barak's proportionality test—an inquiry that could be characterized as an investigation into substantive rationality—asks whether the harm caused by the government's action is disproportionate to the benefit that might be achieved from it. In other words, even if the government's action served compelling interests and the means used were rationally connected to the pursuit of those interests, and even if those means represented the least restrictive alternative, the government's action will nevertheless be deemed unlawful if the harm it inflicts is disproportionately greater than the gains that it might achieve. There is virtually no trace of this aspect of the proportionality test in the doctrine of the U.S. Supreme Court, certainly not in the national security context, and yet Justice Barak routinely and successfully applied it in a wide range of cases in which fundamental values were at stake.

In fact, the substantive branch of the proportionality test was the linchpin of Barak's opinion in the case of the security fence. Although he accepted the military's claim that its proposed line for the security fence would be the most effective in saving the lives of Israeli citizens and that any redrawing of the line would result in increased loss of life from terrorist attacks, he nonetheless ordered sections of the fence be built along a different line in order to reduce the harm to Palestinians that would result from the division of their communities and the separation from their fields and places of work. The harm of the lines proposed by the military was deemed disproportionate to any security advantages that might be achieved. Put another way, Barak was prepared to sacrifice the military objectives of minimizing the risk to Israeli lives in order to avoid the greater harm to the Palestinian communities that would have resulted from the erection of the security barrier as originally planned. His intention was not to demean the importance of the military objective but to find a way to accommodate two compelling, albeit conflicting, values.

In all this—his refusal to defer to the military in the tradeoff of values, his insistence on the least restrictive alternative, and his requirement that the harm to fundamental values not be disproportionate to the gain in security—Barak held firm in his attachment to the law and the belief that the law is the embodiment of reason in the service of humanity. His method was to demand, systematically and relentlessly, that any sacrifices of rights be fully and rationally justified. In so doing, Barak revealed a deep and profound commitment to reason, the common element that unites his life as a professor and as a judge and that accounts for his unique place in Israeli society and in the world legal community. For him to declare, as he has done on many occasions, that "law is everywhere" is to invite us to imagine that every aspect of our public life, even war, can and should be governed by reason, and reason alone.

Aharon Barak and I are the closest of friends and over the years I have often wondered to myself how remarkable it is that in such a small corner of the world, so often racked by violence and religious passions, a modern-day apostle of the Enlightenment rose to take a place not just in the history of Israel but in the history of all mankind.

CODA

Toiling in Eden

Grown men should never confess their love in public, especially when it is the love of an institution; even worse, a law school. But one breach of this edict might be forgiven when, as here, the feelings are so strong and thus so difficult to suppress, and when these feelings must already be evident to the careful reader.

I was interviewed for a position at Yale on two occasions. The second came in the spring of 1974 when I was teaching at Chicago and eventually led to my decision to join the Yale faculty. The other round of interviews occurred some years earlier, in the spring of 1966, while I was finishing my clerkship with Justice Brennan and shortly before I accepted a position at the Civil Rights Division of the Department of Justice. The first set of interviews began at the home of the new dean, Louis Pollak.

A number of the faculty were present at Pollak's. I shook their hands and soon enough was introduced to Ralph Brown. He was a member of the faculty who had co-authored a casebook on copyright with Ben Kaplan, from whom I had taken several courses at Harvard. Standing among his colleagues, Ralph Brown asked the first question—and what a question it was: "Your professors at Harvard say you belong at Yale. What do they mean by that?"

When I began teaching at Chicago in 1968, I was assigned to teach a course that until then had been called "Equity." I had just emerged from a two-year stint at the Civil Rights Division, where I was exposed to the most intense, complicated forms of litigation that had ever taken place under the equity jurisdiction of the federal courts. So, in response to my new assignment, I reflected on that experience and eagerly put together a course I called "Injunctions." Phil Neal, the Dean of Chicago, found this course title unacceptable. He controlled the catalogue and insisted that I call the course "Equitable Remedies," a title that mystified my students since, to all appearances, I knew of only one equitable remedy.

In moving to Yale, I was anticipating another go-round over the title of the course with the Dean, Abe Goldstein, the most commanding dean under whom I ever served. Much to my surprise, though, in keeping with the school's traditions, he expressed complete disinterest in the subject. So, after teaching for six years and after having published a casebook on the subject, I finally was allowed to give my course the name I wanted.

Bruce Ackerman also joined the Yale faculty in the summer of 1974. One day soon after we had both arrived in New Haven he asked what course I was teaching in the fall. I proudly said "Injunctions." He then said, in the manner that generations of Yalies have come to know and love, "That's the worst course title I have ever heard. It is completely inappropriate for the Yale Law School. At Yale it must be 'The Activist Judiciary Meets the Bureaucratic State in the Post–New Deal Era.'"

After this encounter, followed by many others of a similar nature, I had a better sense of what to expect from my new colleagues. In the mid-1970s, Paul Simon released an album called "Still Crazy after All These Years," which struck me then, and still strikes me, as an apt character-ization of the faculty. The Yale faculty is indeed crazy, but crazy in the best sense: intellectually restless; unwilling to accept conventional ac-counts of anything; boldly and defiantly crossing all disciplinary bound-aries; and determined to push and push the law, sometimes even beyond all sensible limits. These were the norms of my predecessors—the giants of the Yale Law School—and these were norms that defined the culture of the institution when I arrived. It was this culture, one that prizes above all else the innovative and the idiosyncratic, that has nourished me all these years and helped me understand what it means to be a professor at the Yale Law School.

A community of individuals that is so very strong-minded (surely a euphemism) is likely to spin out of control at any moment. We need a leader, but it has to be one who is capable of governing an anarchy. Here too, I have been fortunate, though throughout my career, alas, I have almost always refused to acknowledge my gratitude to any of my deans.

My love for the Yale Law School is the devotion of the convert, which, as St. Augustine reminds us, is the most passionate love of all. So, for more than forty years I have been an unqualified pain in the neck to each and every dean under whom I served, sending them endless memorandums accusing them of betraying the most sacred traditions of the school. No doubt all of these missives, known in some quarters as "fissiles," wound up in the deans' "circular files," yet they were always received graciously, which of course only egged me on.

One dean, likely desperate to find a way to deal with me and the other self-appointed keepers of the faith, started a practice of calling each faculty member on his or her birthday and singing "Happy Birthday," with a few refrains in Italian. Can you imagine? A law school governed by a dean who sang "Happy Birthday" to each member of his faculty and who continued this practice decades after he left office and became a federal judge.

A foundational principle of the Yale Law School, often propounded by Joe Goldstein, holds that it is the responsibility of each faculty member to decide what is educationally required, and that it is the responsibility of the Dean to find the funds to support those decisions. This principle may strike the fiscally responsible as bizarre, as indeed it is, but it makes perfect sense in an institution that prizes the autonomy of each individual faculty member and demands that this autonomy be used in bold and inventive ways, unchecked by decanal or even peer review.

Guided by this precept, Abe Goldstein funded the Legal Theory Workshop in an instant when Bruce Ackerman and I proposed it in 1974. This precept was also honored with abundance by Guido Calabresi and Tony Kronman during their deanships as I became increasingly curious about foreign legal systems, and my interests began to shift from civil to human rights. In 1993, Calabresi supported the establishment of a student exchange program—known as Linkages—with a number of Latin American law schools. Once Kronman took over, in July 1994, the reins of the Law School, he endorsed the enlargement of this exchange program to include an ongoing faculty seminar (the *Seminario en Latinoamérica de Teoría Constitucional y Política*—SELA). At roughly the same time, Kronman established the Middle East Legal Studies Seminar (MELSS), modeled after SELA, and launched the Global Constitutionalism Seminar. These ambitious, maybe even extravagant international projects have been at the center of my attention in recent years and, after more than twenty years, are now taken-for-granted fixtures of the Law School.

I am also immensely grateful to my students for the opportunity to be one of their teachers, grateful both for their brilliance and for their attitude toward learning. I have been moved by their willingness to discard their preconceptions of what law is or might be and to fully engage with the lessons of the day—at first bewildered, maybe resistant, but also open and indulgent and finally stirred to forge for themselves an entirely new stance on the law. They quickly became comfortable—maybe too comfortable—speaking back; and whenever they did, they transformed classroom exchanges into a learning experience for everyone, including the instructor.

The faculty like to poke fun at one another. In that spirit we often remark, usually as part of the faculty recruitment process, that the best thing about the Yale Law School is the students. This is meant to be a self-deprecating joke, but it has a kernel of truth. Muneer Ahmad, as a relatively new addition to the faculty, acknowledged the truth of this joke and reformulated it eloquently. The specialness of Yale Law students, he once said, derives from the fact that they do not feel burdened by the law, but rather tend to see themselves as masters of it, and as such entitled to reshape the law in ways that will make it a more perfect instrument of justice.

In the fall of 2010, for roughly the fortieth time, I taught first-year procedure. I had decided to retire at the end of the academic year, so it was the last time I taught the course. The students sensed the end was near, and once they did, I was invited by one group of students, then another, then another, and so on, to have drinks late in the afternoon at Mory's. These were special occasions. They allowed for an intimacy never achievable in a lecture hall. Students asked about different phases of my career, inquired delicately about my family life, and probed my more heretical views on procedure. The french fries were great.

At one of these gatherings a student turned to me and asked with startling directness and simplicity: "Professor Fiss, what is your proudest achievement?" I paused for a second, scrolling in my mind's eye my list of publications, and then I suddenly realized that the answer lay in an entirely different domain. I answered with remarkable clarity and firmness, "You."

Yes, my students are my proudest achievement. They are the ones that have been at the center of my professional life. They are the ones for whom I write. They are the ones I had in mind as I sat in the library each morning preparing for class. They are the ones with whom I was in conversation in the still hours of the morning as I lay half-awake imagining how the afternoon's class will unfold. They are the ones I am often thinking about, sometimes even when my grandchildren tug on my sleeves. They are the ones I count on to realize my deepest dreams and hopes for the law.

I have devoted my professional life to making the world a little bit more just, but always with a clear understanding that as a teacher I will only fully achieve this purpose through my students. When they go forth into the world, I hope they remember that they carry not only their dreams and those of their families and parents, but also those of their teachers.

I realize that this is a difficult time to achieve these larger purposes; so much of the law is in shambles and needs to be righted, for, sadly, we live so far short of our ideals. The challenge before today's generation is staggering, but perhaps even in this endeavor Yale may have one more lesson to teach—a lesson first told to me by Grant Gilmore.

Grant Gilmore was one of the greatest teachers of the Yale Law School. His subject was contracts, specifically Article 9 of the Uniform Commercial Code. He had visited Harvard when I was a student there, and as it happened was on the Chicago faculty when I first joined it in 1968. His time at Chicago was a short, self-imposed exile. He returned to Yale in the early 1970s, and I soon followed him. Once, while visiting at Harvard, Grant was pressed to define the difference between Harvard and Yale; in response, he said that the essential difference was a frame of mind or attitude toward the law. At Harvard the golden age is always the present, but at Yale, Grant said, the golden age lies in the past and will rise once again in the future.

For me, the golden age of American law began on May 17, 1954, and continued until the mid-1970s, when a newly constituted Supreme Court began its disheartening project of denying the redemptive possibilities and promise of *Brown v. Board of Education*. I came to Yale as this process of retrenchment began and lived out my career in an era of American law that is, as I so often declared in class, anything but golden. Yet I know—I know in my heart of hearts—that someday soon the golden age of American law will once again come into being and will be carried on the shoulders of a new generation, determined to turn the lessons they have learned in the classroom into a living truth.

Sources and Acknowledgments

Index

Sources and Acknowledgments

Chapter 1, "Thurgood Marshall: The Law's Promise," depicts personal experiences with Marshall that were initially recounted in "A Vision of the Constitution," *Harvard Civil Rights-Civil Liberties Law Review* 13 (1978): 243–246, reprinted in *Maryland Law Review* 40 (1981): 401–404; "Tribute to Justice Thurgood Marshall," *Harvard Law Review* 105 (1991): 49–55; and "Tribute to Justice Marshall," Special Session of the United States Court of Appeals for the Second Circuit Honoring the Memory of Justice Thurgood Marshall, 995 F.2d xcix (1993). The chapter also draws on familiar stories of Marshall's life contained in Juan Williams, *Thurgood Marshall: American Revolutionary* (New York: Random House, 1998).

Chapter 2, "William Brennan: A Life Lived Twice," presents an account of Brennan's career on the Supreme Court that was first adumbrated in an essay, of the same title, published in *Yale Law Journal* 100 (1991): 1117–1129, later republished in Roger Goldman and David Gallen, *Justice William J. Brennan, Jr.: Freedom First* (New York: Carroll and Graf Publishers, 1994): 63–78. The new challenges facing Brennan in the 1970s and 1980s were described in "The Rehnquist Court: A Return to the Antebellum Constitution," an article coauthored with Charles Krauthammer in *The New Republic*, March 10, 1982.

Chapter 3, "John Doar: To Stand for What Is Right," began as an address at a memorial service for Doar held at Princeton University on January 24, 2015. Doar's own account of his career can be found in a public interview that I conducted with him in October 2012, eventually published in "Voices of the Civil Rights Division: Then and Now," *McGeorge Law Review* 44 (2013): 293–308. A fuller description of the Neshoba trial can be found in Douglas O. Linder, "Bending Toward Justice: John Doar and the 'Mississippi Burning' Trial," *Mississippi Law Journal* 72 (2002): 731–779. A brief biographical note of mine on Doar can be found in *The Yale Biographical Dictionary of American Law*, ed. Roger K. Newman (New Haven, CT: Yale University Press, 2009), 167–168.

Chapter 4, "Burke Marshall: A Reluctant Hero," in part describes Marshall's role as the head of the Civil Rights Division during the early 1960s. My understanding of his leadership of the Division was greatly enriched by Taylor Branch, *Parting the Waters: America in the King Years 1954–63* (New York: Simon and Schuster, 1988); Patricia M. Wald, " 'To Feel the Great Forces': The Times of Burke Marshall," *Yale Law Journal* 105 (1995): 611–620; and John Lewis, "Burke," *Yale Law Journal* 105 (1995): 621–622. The chapter also describes my personal relationship with Marshall and his role on the Yale Law faculty and for that purpose draws on my essay "Not with Our Tears," *Yale Law Journal* 113 (2004): 797–802. An interview in 2015 with a colleague, John Simon, helped me to reconstruct the unusual sequence of events that led to Marshall's Yale appointment in 1970.

Chapter 5, "Harry Kalven: A Tenth Justice," is informed by the close relationship that I developed with Kalven while I taught at the University of Chicago from 1968 to 1974. Reflections on this relationship were first published in "Kalven's Way," *University of Chicago Law Review* 43 (1975): 4–7. The chapter also discusses Kalven's contribution to free speech doctrine, which is largely informed by my work, spanning almost fifteen years, on the manuscript, eventually published as *A Worthy Tradition: Freedom of Speech in America*, ed. Jamie Kalven (New York: Harper & Row, 1988), that he had left upon his death. An Editor's Afterword (pages 589–610) describes my role in the process of preparing the manuscript for publication. A critical perspective on Kalven's celebration on the free speech tradition in the United States is presented in "Free Speech and Social Structure," an essay that appears as chapter 1 of my *Liberalism Divided* (Boulder, CO: Westview Press, 1996).

Chapter 6, "Eugene Rostow: The Law according to Yale," extends an appreciation of the philosophy governing the Yale Law School that was initially presented in a chapter, of the same title, in *Power and Policy in Quest of Law: Essays in Honor of Eugene Victor Rostow*, ed. Myres S. McDougal and W. Michael Reisman (Dordrecht, The Netherlands: Martinus Nijhoff, 1985), 417–424, republished in Spanish as "El Derecho Según Yale," in *La Enseñanza del Derecho y el Ejercicio de la Abogacía*, ed. Martin F. Böhmer (Barcelona: Editorial Gedisa, 1999), 25–34. This chapter also seeks to link Rostow's views of legal education to his more general philosophy of law, as set forth in "The Democratic Character of Judicial Review," *Harvard Law Review* 66 (1952): 193–224, and later in his book *The Ideal in Law* (Chicago: University of Chicago Press, 1978).

Chapter 7, "Arthur Leff: Making Coffee and Other Duties of Citizenship," describes the special role that Leff played in the life of the Yale Law School during one of its most turbulent periods. This phase of the Law School's history is portrayed in Laura Kalman, *Yale Law School and the Sixties: Revolt and Reverberations* (Chapel Hill: University of North Carolina Press, 2005); Laura Kalman, "The Dark Ages," in *History of the Yale Law School: The Tercentennial Lectures*, ed. Anthony T. Kronman (New Haven, CT: Yale University Press, 2004), 154–237; and the "Critical Legal Studies Symposium," *Stanford Law Review* 36 (1984): 1-673. The chapter also revisits themes about the collegial life in the Law School that were initially described in my article of the same title that appeared in *Yale Law Journal* 91 (1981): 224–229.

Chapter 8, "Catharine MacKinnon: Feminism in the Classroom," raises general issues of feminist jurisprudence that I dealt with more systematically in "What Is Feminism?," *Arizona State Law Journal* 26 (1994): 413–428; "Freedom and Feminism," chap. 4, and "The Right Kind of Neutrality," chap. 6, both in *Liberalism Divided* (Boulder, CO: Westview Press, 1996); and *The Irony of Free Speech* (Cambridge, MA: Harvard University Press, 1996). For an assessment of my stance on two other intellectual movements that arose during the 1970s, Critical Legal Studies and Law and Economics, see Laura Kalman, *The Strange Career of Legal Liberalism* (New Haven, CT: Yale University Press, 1998).

Chapter 9, "Joseph Goldstein: The Scholar as Sovereign," depicts Goldstein's role in the Yale Law School and his views about legal education more generally that were initially introduced in "Yale according to Joe," *Yale Law Journal* 110 (2001): 913–916.

Chapter 10, "Carlos Nino: The Death of a Public Intellectual," takes as its point of departure my first trip to Argentina in June 1985. That journey and the relationship with Nino that evolved is the subject of an article, of the same title, that appeared in *Yale Law Journal* 104 (1995): 1187–1200, later republished as a chapter in *Deliberative Democracy and Human Rights*, ed. Harold Hongju Koh and Ronald C. Slye (New Haven, CT: Yale University Press, 1999): 21–30.

Chapter 11, "Robert Cover: Cases and Materials," focuses on the efforts of Cover and myself to revamp the first-year procedure course, an endeavor that was briefly described in my remarks at a memorial service for Cover, published in *Yale Law Journal* 96 (1987): 1717–1723. The broader jurisprudential disagreements between us were aired in a symposium, discussed in this chapter, that was sponsored by the Association of American Law Schools in San Francisco on January 7, 1984. A tape recording of this symposium is available in the Yale Law School library.

Chapter 12, "Morton Horwitz: Timeless Truths," returns to philosophical and political debates that have long divided, and in fact also united, Horwitz and me. These debates are described in an essay of mine with the same title that appeared in *Transformations in American Legal History: Law, Ideology, and Methods: Essays in Honor of Morton J. Horwitz*, ed. Daniel W. Hamilton and Alfred L. Brophy, vol. 2 (Cambridge, MA: Harvard University Press, 2010): 407–421.

Chapter 13, "Aharon Barak: Law Is Everywhere," draws on a tribute of the same title that appeared in *Yale Law Journal* 117 (2007): 256–278, later published in Hebrew in *Bar-Ilan Law Studies* 24 (2008): 351–365; and formed the basis of chapter 5 of *A War Like No Other: The Constitution in a Time of Terror*, ed. Trevor Sutton (New York: The New Press, 2015). These works reflect the growing unease I have had with the failure of the American judiciary to hold the executive and legislative branches of the United States government accountable to the law for their conduct of the War on Terror, and represent an effort to find within Barak's national security rulings a standard to assess this experience.

"Toiling in Eden," the coda of the book, expands on "A Confession," *Yale Law Reports* 58 (2011): 53–55, an address to the Yale Law School class of 2011 upon the occasion of my retirement from the school.

I gratefully acknowledge the contributions of Lawrence Douglas, a friend and professor at Amherst College, for reading an early version of the book and for his help in defining its organization; Ian Malcolm, my editor at Harvard University Press, for his warm embrace of the manuscript, his gracious nudges for revisions, and his stewardship of the production process; Bradley Hayes and Christopher Lombroso, both on the staff of the Yale Law School, for help in locating the photographs and for preparing the manuscript; and Jacob Gelman and Brandon Sadowsky, members of the Yale Law School class of 2018, for careful and insightful research and editorial assistance.

Above all, I am indebted to Daniel Rauch, a member of the Yale Law School class of 2016, for his extraordinary research and editorial assistance. We completed the first essay in January 2015 and worked on the rest of the manuscript for the next year and a half. Throughout, I was buoyed by Dan's curiosity about the figures portrayed here and his capacity to find within the lives of these lawyers important lessons for himself and for his generation.

Index